LETTERHEAD & LOGO DESIGNS 2

CREATING THE CORPORATE IMAGE

ROCKPORT PUBLISHERS • ROCKPORT, MASSACHUSETTS
Distributed by North Light Books • Cincinnati, Ohio

Art Director
Stephen Bridges

Design
Carolyn Letvin

Production Manager
Barbara States

First published in the United States of America by:
Rockport Publishers, Inc.
146 Granite Street
Rockport Massachusetts 01966
Telephone: (508) 546-9590
Fax: (508) 546-7141
Telex: 5106019284 ROCKORT PUB

Distributed to the book trade and art trade in the U.S. and Canada by:
North Light, an imprint of
F & W Publications
1507 Dana Avenue
Cincinnati, Ohio 45207
Telephone: (513) 531-2222

Other distribution by:
Rockport Publishers, Inc.
Rockport, Massachusetts 01966

ISBN 1-56496-006-4

3 5 7 9 10 8 6 4

Printed in Singapore

Procrustes was a fabulous robber of Greek mythology, a giant who enticed travelers into his bed, cutting off the legs or stretching his victims until they fit.

The proliferation of influences on graphic design, the welter of styles and strategies, have spawned an era in which the graphic designer has too often become a Procrustes. Most designers wrangle with the problem of borrowing from the image bank. They feel the imperiative to adapt and shape their work, to balance personal expression and stylistic effect. Yet there is a persistent seduction to produce soulless work sustained only by fragments of styles or past cultures appropriated without real understanding. In effect the assignment is mutilated to fit the bedstead.

To drag out any style or image not related to the job brief is a process yielding only pastiche. As designers we are supposed to navigate the waters of style and function, of pre-packaged solutions and originality, of self-expression and marketing demands. An essential delight of graphic design is that there are few rules. But this notion of borrowing has become tricky. How far can the designer go with arbitrary usage of historical styles and still address the needs of the job? Are there limits to adaptation? The headlong evolution of styles, the development of new technologies compounded by the exigencies of deadlines and client needs mean we cannot avoid occasionally forcing a design problem to recline in a Procrustean bed.

Technique and borrowing reach their limits at the point where real creativity is called for. Kant defined genius as the ability to produce something over and above any rules: genuine creativity has no set recipe. This collection offers evidence that many designers avoid the traps and speak their own honest language, marshaling visual and verbal elements skillfully to speak with force and eloquence. The best of them rescue concepts from Procrustes' bed, preserving intact original meanings as well as originality. Their grammar of design is highly wrought, yet beyond paradigms.

Walter McCord

Walter McCord

Walter McCord runs a one-man design studio in Louisville Kentucky. His work has been recognized by Graphis, AIGA, Idea, Print, New York Art Directors, Communications Arts, Type Directors Club, STA and others, and is in the collection of the Library of Congress.

1. RETAIL

TWIGS

Twigs, Inc.
381 Bleeker Street
New York, New York 10014

TWIGS

Twigs, Inc. 381 Bleeker Street New York, New York 10014 212 620 8188 • 3 World Financial Center New York, New York 10281 212 385 2660

Client: Twigs, Inc.
Design Firm: Lewin/Holland, Inc.
Art Director: Cheryl Lewin
Designer: Cheryl Lewin
Paper/Printing: Four colors

Ronni Michel
164 Beacon Street
Andover, MA 01810
508. 470.3620

164 Beacon Street
Andover, MA 01810

164 Beacon Street
Andover, MA 01810
508.470.3620

Client: Seasons Floral Design
Design Firm: Portfolio
Art Director: Bonnie Mineo
Designer: Busha Husak
Paper/Printing: Two colors on Strathmore Writing

David Fleisher

401 East Cooper Avenue Aspen, Colorado 81611

401 East Cooper Avenue Aspen, Colorado 81611
Tel 303-925-1681 ▲ Fax 303-925-1683

Client: Pitkin Country Dry Goods
Design Firm: Milton Glaser, Inc.
Art Directors: Milton Glaser, David Freedman
Designers: David Freedman, Chi-ming Kan
Paper/Printing: Five colors on Strathmore Writing Laid

Client: Emporio Armani
Design Firm: Anthony McCall Associates
Art Director: Anthony McCall
Designer: Wing Chan
Paper/Printing: One color on French Speckletone

Client: Legacy of Love
Design Firm: Peggy Lauritsen Design
Art Director: Anocha Ghoshachandra
Designer: Anocha Ghoshachandra
Paper/Printing: Two colors on French Speckletone

Client: Presence Fashions
Design Firm: Musser Design
Art Director: Musser
Designer: Musser
Paper/Printing: Three colors on Curtis Brightwater

Client: Cambridge Commercial Carpet
Design Firm: Turpin Design Associates
Art Director: Tony F. Turpin
Designers: Joseph E. Whisnant, Tony F. Turpin
Paper/Printing: One color plus foil on Strathmore Writing Kromekote Cover

Client: Caledonian Inc.
Design Firm: Michael Stanard Inc.
Art Director: Michael Stanard
Designer: Lisa Fingerhut
Paper/Printing: Four colors on Strathmore Writing

Client: Baby ZZZ's/Pawley Island Pub
Design Firm: Mark Palmer Design
Art Director: Mark Palmer
Designer: Mark Palmer
Computer Production: Curtis Palmer
Paper/Printing: Three colors on Strathmore Writing Wove

Client: Jasper Oriental Rugs
Design Firm: McCord Graphic Design
Art Director: Walter McCord
Designer: Walter McCord
Paper/Printing: Tritone plus one color on Neenah Classic Crest

Client: San Francisco Clothing
Design Firm: George Tscherny, Inc.
Art Director: George Tscherny
Designer: George Tscherny

Client: The L·S Collection
Design Firm: Designframe Inc.
Art Director: James A. Sebastian
Designers: James A. Sebastian, John Plunkett, David Reiss, Junko Thomas Schneider
Paper/Printing: Two colors on Curtis Brightwater

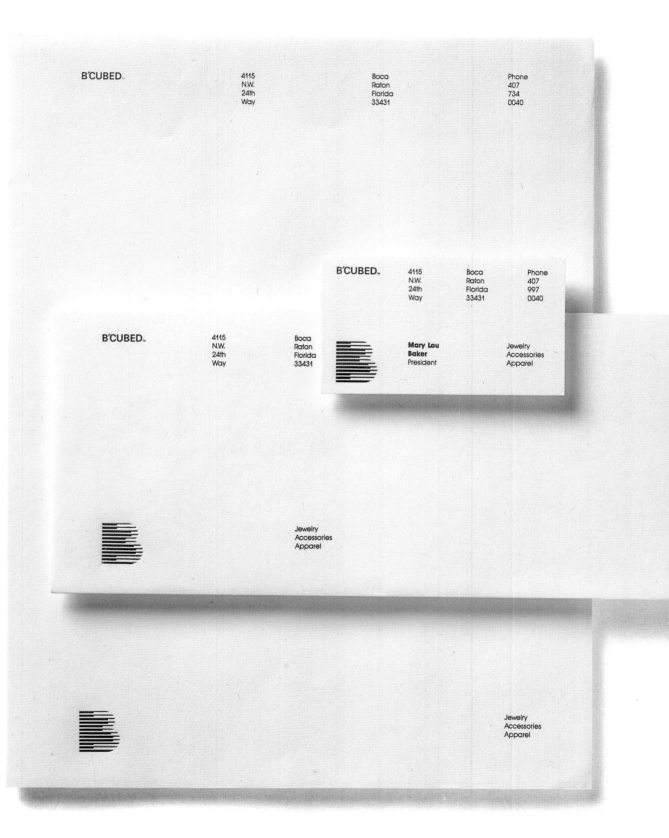

Client: B'Cubed Jewelry
Design Firm: Creative Works
Art Director: Bob Jahn
Designer: Bob Jahn
Illustrator: David Wright
Paper/Printing: Two colors on Strathmore Writing

Client: Gifted Ltd.
Design Firm: Friday Saturday Sunday, Inc.
Designer: Linda Casale
Illustrator: Linda Casale
Paper/Printing: Two colors on Gilbert Oxford

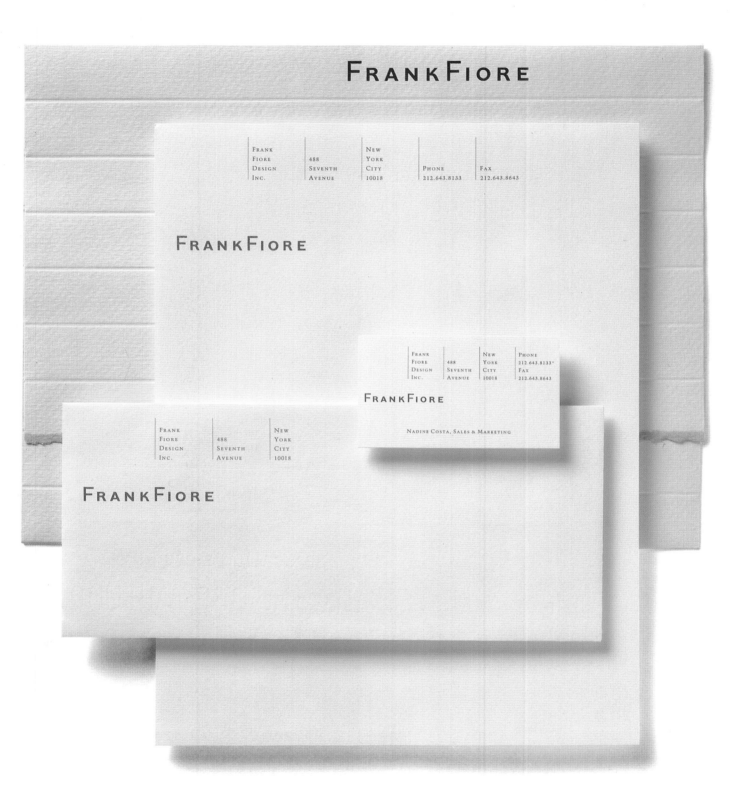

Client: Frank Fiore Design Inc.
Design Firm: Designframe Inc.
Art Director: James A. Sebastian
Designer: Eric Pike
Paper/Printing: One color on Strathmore Writing White Wove

Client: Solo Editions
Design Firm: The Pushpin Group
Art Director: Seymour Chwast
Designer: Greg Simpson

SOUNDEFFECTS

Client: Pilar
Design Firm: Bob Korn Design
Art Director: Bob Korn
Designer: Bob Korn
Illustrator: Bob Korn

Client: Eaglemoor
Design Firm: Hornall Anderson Design Works
Art Director: Jack Anderson
Designers: Jack Anderson, Mary Hermes, David Bates
Illustrator: Nancy Gellos

Client: K2 Corporation
Design Firm: Hornall Anderson Design Works
Art Director: Jack Anderson
Designers: Jack Anderson, David Bates
Illustrator: David Bates

Client: Mother Nature's Gallery
Design Firm: Tollner Design Group
Art Director: Lisa Tollner
Designer: Don Barns
Illustrator: Don Barns

Client: JBL International
Design Firm: Fitch Richardson Smith
Art Director: Ann Gildea
Designers: Kate Murphy, Beth Novitsky

Client: The Tree House
Design Firm: Bob Korn Design
Art Director: Bob Korn
Designer: Bob Korn
Illustrator: Bob Korn

2. FOOD

Client: La Pêche
Design Firm: McCord Graphic Design
Art Director: Walter McCord
Designer: Walter McCord
Illustrator: McCord Graphic Design
Paper/Printing: Letterhead - Two colors on Simpson Gainsborough
Business Card - Four colors on Champion Kromekote

MARK FAHRER • CATERER
43West 13th Street, NYC 10011 • (212) 243-6572

MARK FAHRER • CATERER
43West 13th Street, NYC 10011 • (212) 243-6572

MARK FAHRER • CATERER
43 West 13th Street, NYC 10011 • (212) 243-6572

Client: Mark Fahrer Caterer
Design Firm: Designed To Print + Associates, Ltd.
Art Directors: Tree Trapanese, Peggy Leonard
Designer: Tree Trapanese
Illustrators: Tree Trapanese, Peggy Leonard
Paper/Printing: One color on Strathmore Writing

Client: Broadmoor Baker
Design Firm: Hornall Anderson Design Works
Art Director: Jack Anderson
Designers: Jack Anderson, Mary Hermes
Paper/Printing: One color on Speckletone

CULINARY CONSULTING,
RESTAURANT MANAGEMENT,
& MEDIA RELATIONS

318 E. 70TH STREET
NEW YORK NY 10021
212 249 4721

EPICUS GROUP
318 E. 70TH STREET
NEW YORK NY 10021

STEPHEN KALT

Client: Epicus Group
Design Firm: Lewin/Holland, Inc.
Art Director: Cheryl Lewin
Designer: Cheryl Lewin
Illustrator: Mary Lynn Blasutta

Client: Vinifera Imports
Design Firm: Hornall Anderson Design Works
Art Director: Jack Anderson
Designers: Jack Anderson, David Bates
Illustrator: David Bates
Paper/Printing: Two colors on Tuscan Terra

Client: Bakeries By The Bay
Design Firm: Tharp Did It • Los Gatos/San Francisco
Art Director: Rick Tharp
Designers: Jean Mogannam, Rick Tharp
Paper/Printing: Two colors with copper foil on Simpson Starwhite Vicksburg

Client: The Rockefeller Group
Design Firm: Milton Glaser, Inc.
Art Director: Milton Glaser
Designer: Milton Glaser
Paper/Printing: Four colors on Strathmore Writing Laid

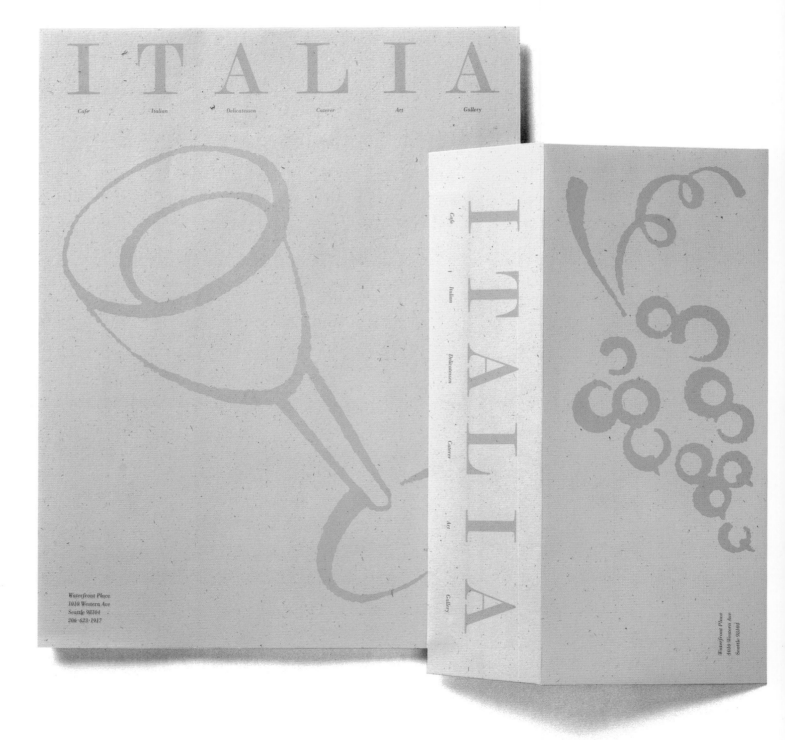

Client: Italia Restaurant
Design Firm: Hornall Anderson Design Works
Art Director: Jack Anderson
Designers: Jack Anderson, Julia LaPine
Paper/Printing: Three colors on Speckletone

Client: 24 Carrot, Inc.
Design Firm: McCord Graphic Design
Art Directors: Walter McCord, Julius Friedman
Designers: Walter McCord, Julius Friedman
Illustrator: Walter McCord
Paper/Printing: Three colors on Strathmore Writing

Client: California Bound
Design Firm: Page Design, Inc.
Art Director: Paul Page
Designer: Tracy Titus
Illustrator: Tracy Titus
Paper/Printing: Four colors on Strathmore Writing

Client: Brooklyn Brewery
Design Firm: Milton Glaser, Inc.
Art Director: Milton Glaser
Designer: Milton Glaser
Paper/Printing: Two colors on Weston Merit Bond

California Grocers Association • P.O. Box 2671 • Sacramento, CA 95812-2671 • Tel: (916) 448-3545 • Fax: (916) 448-2793
1990 Convention And Trade Show • September 15-17, 1990, Anaheim Convention Center

306 SECOND STREET   BROOKLYN, NY 11215   (718) 768-2346

3326 Davidsonville, Rd. Davidsonville, MD 21035 301.798.4051

101 QUEENS DRIVE
KING OF PRUSSIA
PENNSYLVANIA 19406
215-354-0520
FAX: 215-354-0900

Client: Chauncey's Chili
Design Firm: Clark Keller
Art Director: Neal Ashby
Designer: Neal Ashby
Illustrator: Neal Ashby
Paper/Printing: One color on Kraft Speckletone

Client: Mercury Services
Design Firm: Whitney • Edwards Design
Art Director: Charlene Whitney • Edwards
Designer: Charlene Whitney • Edwards
Computer Output: In Tandem Design
Paper/Printing: Two colors on Neenah Classic Laid Writing
Whitestone

Client: Chicago Dog & Deli
Design Firm: Sayles Graphic Design
Art Director: John Sayles
Designer: John Sayles
Paper/Printing: Three colors on Neenah Classic Crest

Client: Peninsula Fountain & Grille
Design Firm: Tharp Did It • Los Gatos/San Francisco
Art Director: Rick Tharp
Designer: Jana Heer, Jean Mogannam, Rick Tharp
Illustrator: Jana Heer
Paper/Printing: Two colors on Simpson EverGreen Recycled

Client: International Candy Corp.
Design Firm: Charrette Inc. Art Department
Art Director: Kevin Sheehan
Designer: Kevin Sheehan
Paper/Printing: Two colors on Strathmore Writing

Client: Mesa Grill
Design Firm: Alexander Isley Design
Art Director: Alexander Isley
Designer: Alexander Knowlton
Paper/Printing: Four colors

California Grocers Association ★ P.O. Box 2671, Sacramento, CA 95812-2671 ★ Tel: (916) 448-3545   Fax: (916) 448-2793
1991 Convention And Trade Show ★ October 12-14, 1991 ★ Reno Convention Center

Client: Sky's The Limit
Design Firm: Page Design, Inc.
Art Director: Paul Page
Designer: Laurel Bigley
Illustrator: Laurel Bigley
Paper/Printing: Four colors on Strathmore Writing

P.O. Box 22146 • 6566 SE Lake Rd • Portland, OR 97222   (503) 652-5600 • (800) 777-3602 • Fax: (503) 652-5699

P.O. Box 22146
6566 SE Lake Rd
Portland, OR 97222-0146

Address Correction Requested

DAN NOVAK
Resident Agent

U.G. Insurance, Inc.
1152 Hartnell Avenue
Redding, California 96002
(916) 223-3470
(800) 547-5973 Ext. 265
Fax: (916) 223-3885

Thank You

U.G. Insurance, Inc. • United Employers Insurance Company • United Rehabilitation Services • U.G.I.C. Ltd.

Client: Grocers Insurance
Design Firm: Robert Bailey Inc.
Art Director: Robert Bailey
Designer: Michael Lancashire
Illustrator: Carolyn Coghlan
Paper/Printing: Five colors on Classic Crest

Client:	Rikki Rikki	**Client:**	American Health Products	**Client:**	Kaplan Hat Co. Restaurant
Design Firm:	Hornall Anderson Design Works	**Design Firm:**	Kollberg/Johnson Associates	**Design Firm:**	J. Brelsford Design, Inc.
Art Director:	Jack Anderson	**Art Director:**	Gary Kollberg	**Art Director:**	Jerry Brelsford
Designers:	Jack Anderson, David Bates, Lian Ng				
Illustrator:	David Bates				

Client:	The Trolley Restaurant	**Client:**	Sisley	**Client:**	Tucker Farm
Design Firm:	Bob Korn Design	**Design Firm:**	Josh Freeman/Associates	**Design Firm:**	Rick Eiber Design (RED)
Art Director:	Bob Korn	**Art Director:**	Josh Freeman, Vickie Sawyer Karten	**Art Director:**	Rick Eiber
Designer:	Bob Korn	**Designer:**	Greg Clarke	**Designer:**	Rick Eiber
Illustrator:	Bob Korn	**Illustrator:**	Greg Clarke	**Illustrator:**	John Fortune

Client: Ralphaels
Design Firm: May Design Associates
Art Director: Frederick Mozzy
Designer: Frederick Mozzy
Illustrator: Frederick Mozzy

Client: Angelica Kitchen
Design Firm: Frank D'Astolfo Design
Art Director: Frank D'Astolfo
Designer: Frank D'Astolfo

Client: Goodie Gram
Art Director: Adam, Filippo & Associates
Design Firm: Adam, Filippo & Associates

Client: Marsh Restaurant
Design Firm: Design Center
Art Director: John C. Reger
Designer: Kobe

Client: Consolidated Restaurants
Design Firm: Hornall Anderson Design Works
Art Director: Jack Anderson
Designers: Jack Anderson, Mary Hermes, David Bates
Illustrators: George Tanagi/Hornall Anderson Design Works

Client: Let The Flower Fly
Design Firm: Design Center
Art Director: John Reger
Designer: Kobe

3. REAL ESTATE

BUCKHEAD PLAZA

BUCKHEAD PLAZA

3060 Peachtree Rd. NW/Atlanta, GA 30305

Leasing & Management by Taylor & Mathis/3060 Peachtree Rd. NW/Atlanta, GA 30305/404-231-0222
A Joint Development of Taylor & Mathis and Metropolitan Life Insurance Company

Client: Taylor & Mathis
Design Firm: Rousso+Associates Inc.
Art Director: Steve Rousso
Designer: Steve Rousso
Illustrator: Steve Rousso

Xerox Realty Corporation
P.O. Box 2000
Route 7 and 659
Leesburg, Virginia 22075
703 478.1013

LANSDOWNE

Xerox Realty Corporation
P.O. Box 2000
Route 7 and 659
Leesburg, Virginia 22075

LANSDOWNE

Client: Xerox Realty Company
Design Firm: Richard Danne & Associates Inc.
Art Director: Richard Danne
Designer: Gary Skeggs
Paper/Printing: Two colors on Simpson Protocol Writing

Client: Rittenhouse Hotel & Condominiums
Design Firm: Katz Wheeler Design
Art Director: Joel Katz
Designer: Joel Katz
Paper/Printing: Two colors on Protocol 100

Client: The Harborside Corporation
Design Firm: Donovan and Green
Art Director: Michael Donovan
Designer: Peter Galperin
Paper/Printing: Two colors on Strathmore Writing Bright White Wove

Polo Fields, Inc.   2309 Watterson Trail   Louisville, Kentucky 40299

Polo Fields, Inc.   2309 Watterson Trail   Louisville, Kentucky 40299   502-266-6001

Client: J.D. Cooper Builder
Design Firm: Sequel, Inc.
Art Director: Denise Olding
Designer: Denise Olding
Illustrator: Denise Olding
Paper/Printing: Three colors on Kimberly Writing Classic Crest Solar White

Client: Center City District
Design Firm: Katz Wheeler Design
Art Director: Joel Katz
Designer: Joel Katz
Paper/Printing: Two colors on Strathmore Renewal

Client: Church Metro
Design Firm: Steve Lundgren Graphic Design
Art Director: Steve Lundgren
Designer: Steve Lundgren
Paper/Printing: Two colors on Neenah Classic Crest

Client: Western Development Corp.
Design Firm: Milton Glaser, Inc.
Art Director: Milton Glaser
Designer: Milton Glaser
Paper/Printing: Two colors on Strathmore Writing Laid

Client: Los Angeles Center
Design Firm: Davies Associates
Art Director: Noel Davies
Designers: Cathy Tetef, Meredith Kamm
Paper/Printing: Two colors and embossing on Crane's Crest

Client: Citygate Associates
Design Firm: Page Design, Inc.
Art Director: Paul Page
Designer: Laurel Bigley
Illustrator: Laurel Bigley
Paper/Printing: Two colors and clear foil on Circa Select

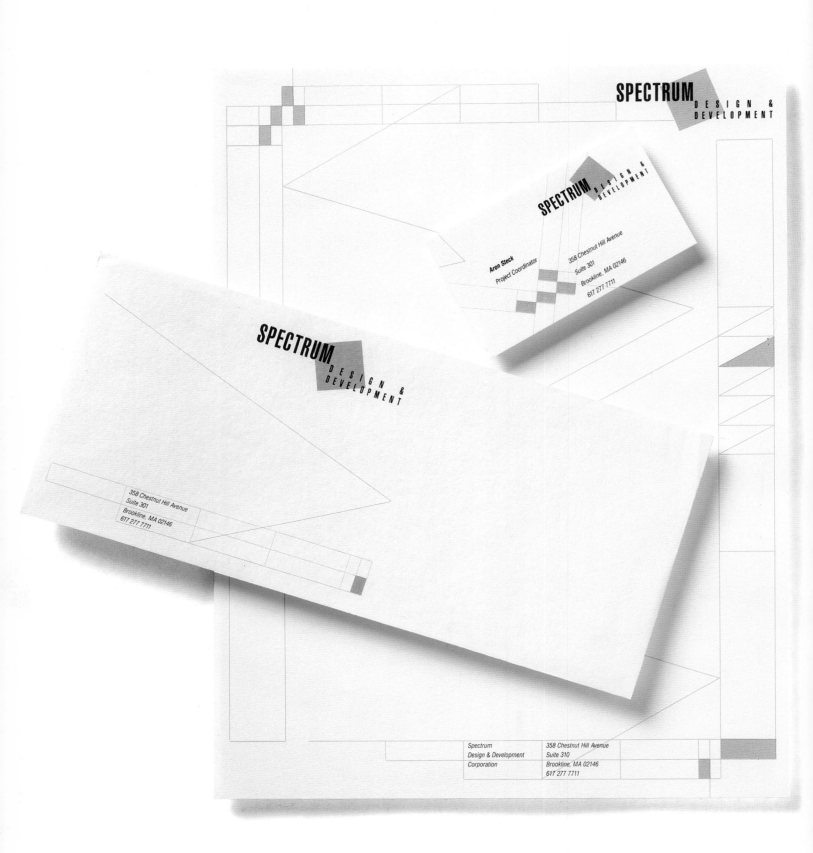

SPECTRUM DESIGN & DEVELOPMENT

SPECTRUM DESIGN & DEVELOPMENT

Aron Steck
Project Coordinator

358 Chestnut Hill Avenue
Suite 301
Brookline, MA 02146

617 277 7711

SPECTRUM DESIGN & DEVELOPMENT

358 Chestnut Hill Avenue
Suite 301
Brookline, MA 02146
617 277 7711

Spectrum
Design & Development
Corporation

358 Chestnut Hill Avenue
Suite 310
Brookline, MA 02146
617 277 7711

Client: Spectrum
Design Firm: Marc English: Design
Art Director: Marc English
Designer: Marc English
Paper/Printing: Two colors on Strathmore Writing

Client: Corporex Center
Design Firm: Michael Aron and Company
Art Director: Michael Aron
Designer: Michael Aron
Paper/Printing: One color on Strathmore Bright White Wove

THE ARBORETUM

THE ARBORETUM

Lisa A. Goldstein

2000 Colorado Ave. ■ Santa Monica, CA 90404 ■ 213/828 5551 ■ Fax 213/315 5071

THE ARBORETUM

2000 Colorado Avenue ■ Santa Monica, California 90404 ■ 213/828 5551 ■ Fax 213/315 5071

Client: Lowe Development Corporation
Design Firm: Josh Freeman/Associates
Art Directors: Josh Freeman, Vickie Sawyer Karten
Designers: Vickie Sawyer Karten, Jennifer Bass
Illustrator: Vickie Sawyer Karten
Paper/Printing: Three colors

Client: ROI Realty Services, Inc.
Design Firm: Integrate, Inc.
Art Directors: John Galvin, Stephen Quinn
Designers: John Galvin, Stephen Quinn
Paper/Printing: Two colors on Gilbert Writing

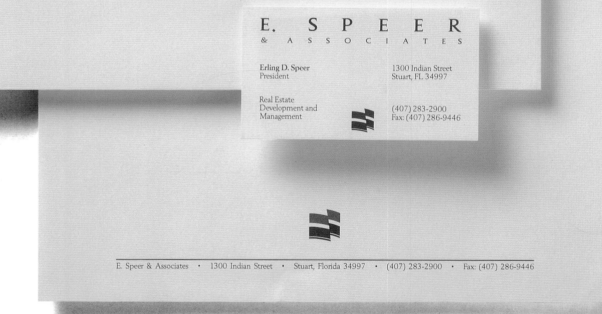

E. SPEER
& ASSOCIATES

E. Speer & Associates · 1300 Indian Street · Stuart, Florida 34997

E. SPEER
& ASSOCIATES

Erling D. Speer
President

1300 Indian Street
Stuart, FL 34997

Real Estate
Development and
Management

(407) 283-2900
Fax: (407) 286-9446

E. Speer & Associates · 1300 Indian Street · Stuart, Florida 34997 · (407) 283-2900 · Fax: (407) 286-9446

Client: E. Speer & Associates
Design Firm: Design/Joe Sonderman, Inc.
Art Director: Tim Gilland
Designer: Andy Crews
Paper/Printing: Three colors on Classic Crest

Client: McDonald Development Company
Design Firm: Turpin Design Associates
Art Director: Tony F. Turpin
Designers: James K. Whitely, Tony F. Turpin

Client: Eastern Columbia Building
Design Firm: Davies Associates
Art Director: Noel Davies
Designers: Cathy Tetef, Meredith Kamm
Paper/Printing: Three colors on Crane's Crest Fluorescent White Wove

Client: Site Research Group
Design Firm: McCord Graphic Design
Art Director: Walter McCord
Designer: Walter McCord
Illustrator: Melvin Prueitt
Paper/Printing: Two colors on Simpson Filare

649 SOUTH BROADWAY SUITE 200, LOS ANGELES, CA 90014 213/624-1900

Site Research Group
20th Floor, Meidinger Tower
The Galleria
Louisville, Kentucky 40202
(502)587-0091

Cash Lewman
Real Estate
1332 Cherokee Road
Louisville, Kentucky 40204
502: 456-4947

THE St. JAMES

CLARK MORTON
PRESIDENT/GENERAL MANAGER

UNCOMPROMISED LIVING: ON THE BEACH, ON LONGBOAT KEY
1245 Gulf of Mexico Drive, Longboat Key, FL 34228, 813-383-6444, FX 813-383-2590

Client: Cash Lewman
Design Firm: McCord Graphic Design
Art Director: Walter McCord
Designer: Walter McCord
Illustrator: Walter McCord
Paper/Printing: Two colors on Strathmore Writing

Client: The St. James Development Co.
Design Firm: Creative Works
Art Directors: David Wright, Bob Jahn
Designer: David Wright, Bob Jahn
Paper/Printing: Two colors on Gilbert Oxford

Continental Development Group Inc.

Continental Development Group Inc.

Continental Development Group Inc.

Richard A. Kahan
Managing Director

488 Madison Avenue
New York, N.Y. 10022
(212) 303-1477

Continental Development Group Inc.

488 Madison Avenue, New York, N.Y. 10022

488 Madison Avenue, New York, N.Y. 10022

Richard A. Kahan, Managing Director, 488 Madison Avenue, New York, N.Y. 10022 (212) 303-1477

Client:	Continental Development Group, Inc.
Design Firm:	Donovan and Green
Art Director:	Michael Donovan
Designer:	Dan Miller
Paper/Printing:	Two colors on Protocol Writing Bright White

Client: Camp Hill Shopping Mall
Design Firm: Musser Design
Art Director: Musser
Designer: Musser
Illustrator: Musser
Paper/Printing: Two colors plus embossing on Curtis Flannel

Client: Bell-Park Condominiums
Design Firm: May Design Associates
Art Director: Frederick Mozzy
Designer: Frederick Mozzy
Illustrator: Frederick Mozzy
Paper/Printing: Two colors and embossing on Gilbert Neu-Tech

MEADŌWGATE

<table>
<tr><td>Client:</td><td>Northwest Building Corporation</td></tr>
<tr><td>Design Firm:</td><td>Hornall Anderson Design Works</td></tr>
<tr><td>Art Director:</td><td>Jack Anderson</td></tr>
<tr><td>Designers:</td><td>Jack Anderson, Cliff Chung, David Bates</td></tr>
<tr><td>Illustrators:</td><td>Bruce Hale, David Bates</td></tr>
</table>

<table>
<tr><td>Client:</td><td>Community Dynamics, Inc.</td></tr>
<tr><td>Design Firm:</td><td>Josh Freeman/Associates</td></tr>
<tr><td>Art Directors:</td><td>Josh Freeman, Vickie Sawyer Karten</td></tr>
<tr><td>Designer:</td><td>Vickie Sawyer Karten</td></tr>
<tr><td>Illustrator:</td><td>Bob Maile</td></tr>
</table>

<table>
<tr><td>Client:</td><td>Bedford Properties</td></tr>
<tr><td>Design Firm:</td><td>Vanderbyl Design</td></tr>
<tr><td>Designer:</td><td>Michael Vanderbyl</td></tr>
</table>

<table>
<tr><td>Client:</td><td>Stern Development</td></tr>
<tr><td>Design Firm:</td><td>Adam, Filippo & Associates</td></tr>
<tr><td>Art Director:</td><td>Robert Adam</td></tr>
<tr><td>Designers:</td><td>Barbara S. Peak, Ralph James Russini</td></tr>
</table>

<table>
<tr><td>Client:</td><td>Oxford Development</td></tr>
<tr><td>Design Firm:</td><td>Adam, Filippo & Associates</td></tr>
<tr><td>Art Director:</td><td>Adam, Filippo & Associates</td></tr>
<tr><td>Designer:</td><td>Ralph James Russini</td></tr>
</table>

<table>
<tr><td>Client:</td><td>The Callison Partnership</td></tr>
<tr><td>Design Firm:</td><td>Hornall Anderson Design Works</td></tr>
<tr><td>Art Director:</td><td>Jack Anderson</td></tr>
<tr><td>Designers:</td><td>Jack Anderson, Mary Hermes</td></tr>
<tr><td>Illustrator:</td><td>Mary Hermes</td></tr>
</table>

4. PROFESSIONAL SERVICES

Client: Sunstone Software
Design Firm: Hornall Anderson Design Works
Art Director: Jack Anderson
Designers: Jack Anderson, Cliff Chung
Paper/Printing: Two colors, gold hot stamp, and blind embossing on Strathmore Writing

Velocity Software
XA Products
and Services for VM

60 Alban Street
Boston, MA 02124

617·825·3599

Velocity Software
60 Alban Street
Boston, MA 02124

Romney White   *Vice President*

Velocity Software
XA Products
and Services for VM

60 Alban Street
Boston, MA 02124

617·825·3599

Client: Velocity Software, Inc.
Design Firm: Unlimited Swan, Inc.
Art Director: Jim Swan
Designer: Rob Swan
Illustrator: Rob Swan
Paper/Printing: Two colors on Strathmore Writing

Client: Blue Sky Systems
Design Firm: McCord Graphic Design
Art Director: Walter McCord
Designers: Walter McCord, Julia Comer
Illustrator: Walter McCord
Paper/Printing: Three colors on Strathmore Writing

Client: Bradley Group
Design Firm: Margo Chase Design
Art Director: Margo Chase
Designer: Margo Chase
Paper/Printing: Three colors on Mohawk Superfine

SERENGETI SOFTWARE
16769 HICKS ROAD
LOS GATOS, CA 95032
PHONE 408.268.0408
FAX 408.268.0847
ALINK: SERENGETI

SERENGETI SOFTWARE
16769 HICKS ROAD
LOS GATOS, CA 95032

MICHAEL R. BURKE
PRESIDENT

SERENGETI SOFTWARE
16769 HICKS ROAD
LOS GATOS, CA 95032
PHONE 408.268.0408
FAX 408.268.0847
ALINK: SERENGETI

S E R E N G E T I ™

S E R E N G E T I ™

Client: Serengeti Software
Design Firm: Tharp Did It • Los Gatos/San Francisco
Art Director: Rick Tharp
Designers: Rick Tharp, Jean Mogannam
Paper/Printing: Three colors on Simpson EverGreen Recycled

Client: Under The Umbrella
Design Firm: Mark Palmer Design
Art Director: Mark Palmer
Designer: Mark Palmer
Computer Production: Curtis Palmer
Paper/Printing: Two colors on Classic Crest Wove

Client: Incrementum, Inc.
Design Firm: Richard Danne & Associates
Art Director: Richard Danne
Designer: Richard Danne
Paper/Printing: Two colors on Simpson Protocol Writing

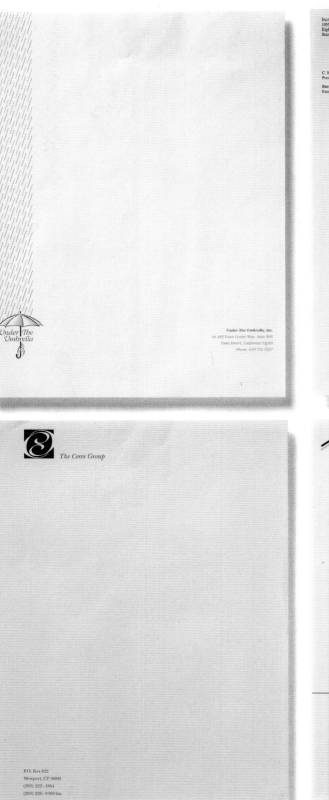

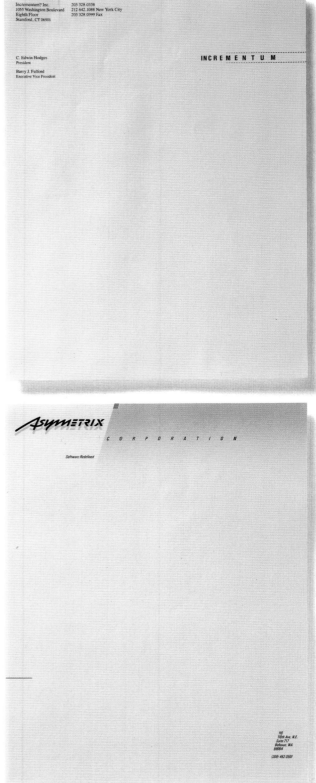

Client: The Ceres Group
Design Firm: Flagg, Brothers Inc.
Designer: Richard Scalzo, Jr.
Illustrator: Richard Scalzo, Jr.
Paper/Printing: Two colors on Neenah Environment

Client: Asymetrix Corporation
Design Firm: Hornall Anderson Design Works
Art Director: Jack Anderson
Designers: Jack Anderson, Greg Walters
Calligrapher: Bruce Hale
Paper/Printing: Four colors on Strathmore Writing

Client: Vulcan Ventures
Design Firm: Hornall Anderson Design Works
Art Director: Jack Anderson
Designers: Jack Anderson, Mary Hermes
Paper/Printing: Four colors on Strathmore Writing

COMPUTER TRAINING SYSTEMS

103 Providence Mine Rd., #202

Nevada City, California 95959

(916) 265-0300

FAX (916) 265-6550

COMPUTER TRAINING SYSTEMS

103 Providence Mine Rd., #202

Nevada City, California 95959

Client: ComTrain
Design Firm: LeeAnn Brook Design
Art Director: LeeAnn Brook
Designer: LeeAnn Brook
Paper/Printing: Two colors on Strathmore Writing

EMMES

EMMES

Michael Sonnenfeldt
President

Emmes & Co., Inc.
62 Park Street
Tenafly, NJ 07670

Mailing address:
P.O. Box 549
Tenafly, NJ 07670

Tel: 201·871·4030
Fax: 201·871·0024

EMMES

Emmes & Co., Inc.
P.O. Box 549
Tenafly, NJ 07670

Michael Sonnenfeldt	Emmes & Co., Inc.	Mailing address:	Tel: 201·871·4030
President	62 Park Street	P.O. Box 549	Fax: 201·871·0024
	Tenafly, NJ 07670	Tenafly, NJ 07670	

Client: Emmes and Company
Design Firm: Donovan and Green
Art Director: Nancye Green
Designer: Clint Morgan
Paper/Printing: Two colors and blind embossing on Crane's Crest Fluorescent White

Client: Colorcurve Systems Inc.
Design Firm: Designframe Inc.
Art Director: James A. Sebastian
Designer: James A. Sebastian, John Plunkett, Frank Nichols
Paper/Printing: Seven colors on Simpson Starwhite Vicksburg Tiara Text Vellum

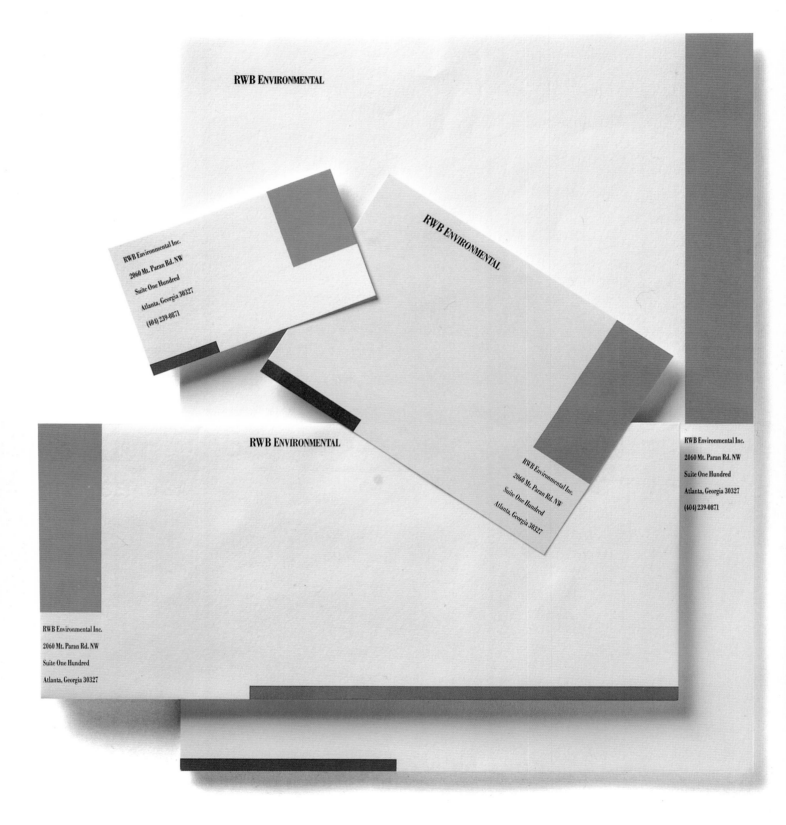

Client: RWB Environmental
Design Firm: Rousso+Associates Inc.
Art Director: Steve Rousso
Designer: Steve Rousso
Paper/Printing: Three colors on Strathmore Writing

RENAISSANCE PARTNERS

306 Plaza Building

Yost Boulevard

Pittsburgh, PA 15221

(412) 829-2588

RENAISSANCE PARTNERS

306 Plaza Building

Yost Boulevard

Pittsburgh, PA 15221

Client: Renaissance Partners
Design Firm: Adam, Filippo & Associates
Art Director: Robert Adam
Designer: Adam, Filippo & Associates
Paper/Printing: Two colors on Crane's Distaff Linen White Laid

One Hillendale Road
Perkasie, PA 18944
215.453.3022

Blake H. Eisenhart
General Auditor

Independence Bancorp

Independence Bancorp

One Hillendale Road
Perkasie, PA 18944

One Hillendale Road
Perkasie, PA 18944
215.453.3049

Independence Bancorp

John T. Blough

Corporate Officer
Treasury Division

Client: Independence Bancorp
Design Firm: Katz Wheeler Design
Art Director: Alina R. Wheeler
Designer: Dan Picard
Paper/Printing: Two colors and embossing on Protocol Writing

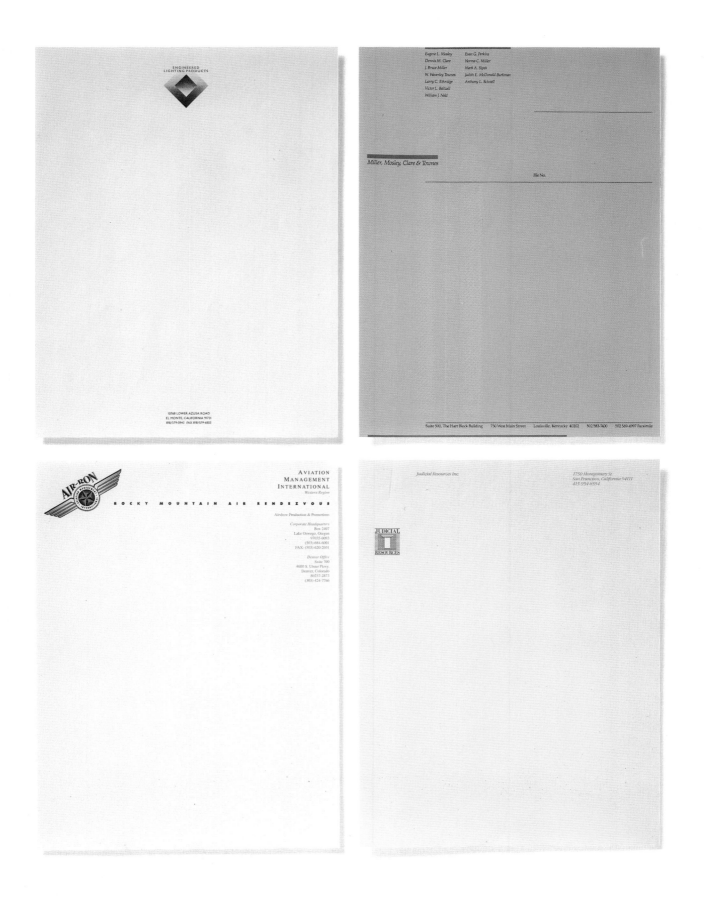

Client: Aviation Management International
Design Firm: Robert Bailey, Inc.
Designer: John Williams
Paper/Printing: Two colors and foil on Classic Crest

Client: Judicial Resources Inc.
Design Firm: Cognata Associates
Art Director: Richard Cognata
Designer: Richard Cognata
Paper/Printing: Two colors

Client: Wall Street Advisors
Design Firm: Design Center
Art Director: John Reger
Designer: Todd Spichke
Paper/Printing: Four colors

A R E N A   D E R H O H A N N E S I A N   &   A S S O C I A T E S

A R E N A   D E R H O H A N N E S I A N   &   A S S O C I A T E S

A R E N A   D E R H O H A N N E S I A N   &   A S S O C I A T E S

26 Towle Farm Rd., Suite 14, Hampton, NH 03842

26 Towle Farm Rd., Suite 14
Hampton, NH 03842
Tel: 603.926.4007 Fax: 603.929.1425

26 Towle Farm Rd., Suite 14
Hampton, NH 03842
Tel: 603.926.4007
Fax: 603.929.1425

Master Planning
Selection Process Planning
Terminal Planning
ARFF/Emergency Planning
Security Planning

A R E N A   D E R H O H A N N E S I A N
&   A S S O C I A T E S

Charles T. Arena
Senior Partner

183 State, St., 7th Floor
Boston, MA 02109
Tel: 617.523.3700 Fax: 617.523.5969

Client: Arena Derhohannesian
Design Firm: Cipriani Kremer Design
Art Director: Robert Cipriani
Paper/Printing: Two colors on Crane's Crest

Client: Arbor Systems Group
Design Firm: Perich + Partners
Art Director: Ernie Perich
Designers: Janine Thielk, Steve Atkinson
Paper/Printing: Two colors

LANE POWELL MOSS & MILLER

RAYMOND W. HAMAN, P.S.
G. KEITH GRIM, P.S.
D. WAYNE GITTINGER
BARRY H. BIGGS
RICHARD F. ALLEN, P.S.
ROBERT W. THOMAS
HARTLEY PAUL
DAVID C. LYCETTE
ROBERT J. FREDERICK, P.S.
JOHN R. TOMLINSON
FRANK W. DRAPER
ROBERT L. ISRAEL, P.S.
ROBERT R. DAVIS, JR.
EUGENE R. NIELSON
DALE E. KREMER, P.S.
CHARLES R. EKBERG, P.S.
KENYON P. KELLOGG, P.S.
MICHAEL O. DWYER
MARK EDWIN JOHNSON
JAMES L. ROBART*
C. WILLIAM BAILEY
EVAN O. THOMAS III
MICHAEL E. MORGAN
KERMIT E. BARKER, JR.**
WAYNE W. HANSEN
JAMES B. STOETZER*
RICHARD C. SIEFERT
LARRY S. GANGNES, P.S.
MICHAEL L. COHEN, P.S.
DAVID G. JOHANSEN
MICHAEL H. RUNYAN
DEBORAH D. WRIGHT
DALE W. HOUSE**
ANNE MCDONALD
H. PETER SORG, JR.

Law Offices

Evergreen Plaza
Building
711 Capitol Way
Olympia, WA
98501-1231

(206) 754-6001

Facsimile:
(206) 754-1605

A Partnership
Including
Professional
Corporations

LANE POWELL MOSS & MILLER

1420 Fifth Ave.
Suite 4100
Seattle, WA
98101-2338

LANE POWELL MOSS & MILLER

1420 Fifth Ave.
Suite 4100
Seattle, WA
98101

(206) 223-7000

Telex: 32-8808
Facsimile:
(206) 223-7107

Patricia H. Welch
Attorney at Law

Seattle, WA
Anchorage, AK
Bellevue, WA
Mount Vernon, WA
Olympia, WA
London, England

MICHAEL K. NAVE
JOHN R. NEELEMAN*
MICHAEL A. NESTEROFF
CHRISTIAN N. OLDHAM
JOHN E.D. POWELL
ALBERT M. RAINES
D. MICHAEL REILLY
ELIZABETH A. RICHARDSON
CHERYLL RUSSELL
MARK P. SCHEER**
DAVID M. SCHOEGGL
RICHARD W. SEARS
DOUGLAS E. SMITH
STEPHEN C. SMITH
DAVID C. SPELLMAN
CATHY A. SPICER
LAWRENCE W. STEVENS
PAUL D. SWANSON
COLEEN D. THOMPSON
THOMAS W. TOP
KAREN VEDDER
TIM D. WACKERBARTH
JAMES P. WAGNER**
RAYMOND S. WEBER
BRUCE P. WEILAND
PATRICIA H. WELCH
WM. BRADFORD WELLER
DOUGLAS E. WHEELER
MARK WHEELER
BRUCE WINCHELL
MARY ELLEN ZALEWSKI*

COUNSEL TO THE FIRM
WILBUR J. LAWRENCE
EUGENE H. KNAPP, JR.
JEFFREY D. GOLTZ

OF COUNSEL
GEORGE V. POWELL
BRUCE SHORTS
WILLIAM J. WALSH, JR.
GORDON W. MOSS

* ADMITTED IN ALASKA
** ADMITTED IN ALASKA
AND WASHINGTON
ALL OTHERS ADMITTED
IN WASHINGTON

Client: Lane Powell Moss & Miller
Design Firm: Hornall Anderson Design Works
Art Director: Jack Anderson
Designers: Jack Anderson, Mary Hermes, Juliet Shen
Paper/Printing: One color on Protocol Writing

MOSS·ADAMS

CERTIFIED PUBLIC ACCOUNTANTS

1001 - 4th Avenue, Suite 2830
Seattle, Washington 98154-1199

Phone 206.223.1820
FAX 206.622.9975

Offices in Principal Cities of
Washington, Oregon and California
Internationally, Moores Rowland Intl.

ARLENE PAULSON

MOSS·ADAMS

Administrative Office

1001 - 4th Ave., Suite 2830
Seattle, WA 98154-1106

Phone 206.223.1820
FAX 206.622.9975

MOSS·ADAMS

Client: Moss Adams
Design Firm: Rick Eiber Design (RED)
Art Director: Rick Eiber
Designer: Rick Eiber
Paper/Printing: Two colors on Classic Crest

DAVIS
The Davis Company

DAVIS
The Davis Company

1400 K Street, Suite 311 Sacramento, CA 95814

DAVIS
The Davis Company

Michael M. Davis

1400 K Street, Suite 311 Sacramento, CA 95814
916.444.6150 FAX 916.447.4011

1400 K Street, Suite 311 Sacramento, CA 95814
916.444.6150 FAX 916.447.4011

Client: The Davis Company
Design Firm: Marketing By Design
Art Director: Joel Stinghen
Designer: Joel Stinghen
Illustrator: Joel Stinghen
Paper/Printing: Two colors on Protocol Writing

PRO_MOTION_

72-880
Fred Waring Drive
Suite D-17
Palm Desert, CA
92260
(619) 346-2253
FAX (619) 346-7133

72-880
Fred Waring Drive
Suite D-17
Palm Desert, CA
92260

72-880
Fred Waring Drive
Suite D-17
Palm Desert, CA
92260
(619) 346-2253
FAX (619) 346-7133

SILVIA STABILE
Marketing Director

Client:	Promotion
Design Firm:	Mark Palmer Design
Art Director:	Mark Palmer
Designer:	Mark Palmer
Paper/Printing:	Two colors on Strathmore Writing Laid

Client: Lincx Inc.
Design Firm: Michael Stanard Inc.
Art Director: Michael Stanard
Designers: Michael Stanard, Marcos Chavez
Paper/Printing: Two colors on Strathmore Writing

Client: Atlantic Mutual Companies
Design Firm: Richard Danne & Associates Inc.
Art Director: Richard Danne
Designer: Eric Atherton
Paper/Printing: Two colors on Strathmore Writing

LINCX

Two North Park Suite 600
2000 Park Lane
Dallas, Texas 75231
214.340.3400

AtlanticMutual Companies

Atlantic Mutual Insurance Company
Centennial Insurance Company
430 Mountain Avenue
Murray Hill, New Jersey 07974
201 771.0660

MANHATTAN MANAGED
FUTURES, INC.

1285 Avenue of the Americas
35th Floor
New York, NY 10019
212-237-2828

SUMMIT

RISK MANAGEMENT &
INSURANCE SERVICES,
INCORPORATED

Principals:
Theodore L.K. Yeh, Jr., ARM
Jim G. DeLeria
André J. Olson
Cheryl A. Downey
Marlene Suphmann

P.O. Box 255097
Sacramento, CA 95865
455 University Ave, Suite 100
Sacramento, CA 95825
(916) 649-8500
FAX (916) 649-0940
(800) 444-2729

Client: Manhattan Managed Futures
Design Firm: Stark Design Associates
Art Director: Adriane Stark
Designer: Adriane Stark
Paper/Printing: Two colors on Strathmore Writing

Client: Summit Risk Management
Design Firm: Marketing By Design
Art Director: Joel Stinghen
Designer: Joel Stinghen
Illustrator: Joel Stinghen
Paper/Printing: Two colors on Gilbert Writing

Client: Big Sky Limited Partnership
Design Firm: Identity Center
Art Director: Wayne Kosterman
Designer: John Anderson
Paper/Printing: Two colors

McIntyre Rowan
Executive Recruitment & Selection

415 Yonge Street

Suite 1101

Toronto, Ontario

M5B 2E7

Tel 416.598.8838

Fax 416.598.3088

McIntyre Rowan
Executive Recruitment & Selection

415 Yonge Street

Suite 1101

Toronto, Ontario M5B 2E7

McIntyre Rowan
Executive Recruitment & Selection

415 Yonge Street

Suite 1101

Toronto, Ontario M5B 2E7

Tel 416.598.8838

Fax 416.598.3088

Lawrence Foerster, B.A., C.P.C.
Partner

Client: McIntyre Rowan
Design Firm: Burns Connacher & Waldron
Art Director: Nat Connacher
Designers: Nat Connacher, Maria Carluccio
Illustrator: Nat Connacher
Paper/Printing: Two colors on Strathmore Writing

CHARLES R. DRUMMOND

17095 Crescent Drive

Los Gatos, CA 95030

408.354.3387

Strategic Communications

Client: Drummond Strategic Communications
Design Firm: Tharp Did It • Los Gatos/San Francisco
Art Directors: Rick Tharp, Charles Drummond
Designers: Rick Tharp, Thom Marchionna
Paper/Printing: Two colors and foil embossing on Simpson Protocol

Client: Thurston Accounting
Design Firm: Mace Messier Design Associates
Art Director: Marilyn Messier
Designer: Christopher Pallotta
Illustrator: Christopher Pallotta
Paper/Printing: Two colors on Strathmore Bond

Client: Boulder Business and Professional Women
Design Firm: Pollman Marketing Arts Inc.
Art Director: Jennifer Pollman
Designers: Jennifer Davis, Jeanine Menefee
Paper/Printing: Two colors on Passport Recycled Text #80 Gypsum

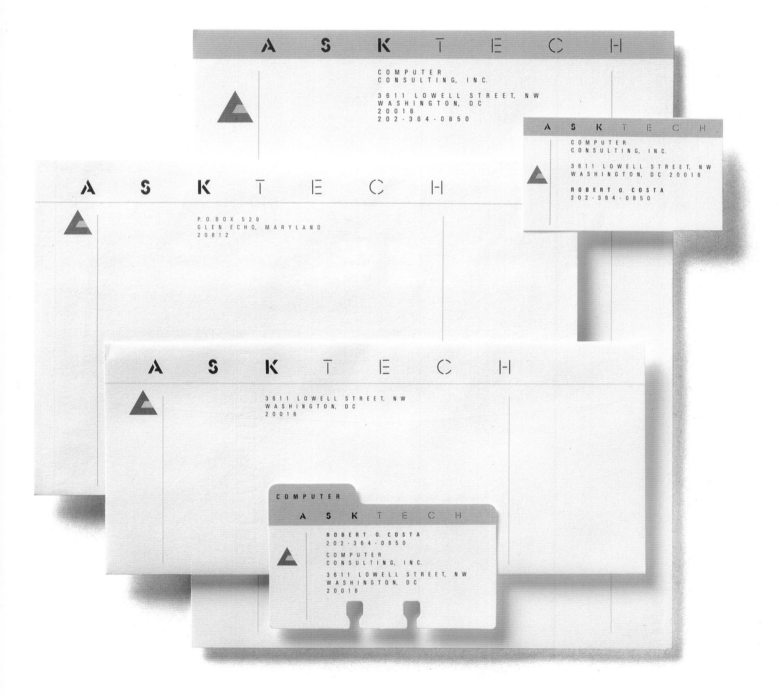

Client: Ask Tech Computer Consulting
Design Firm: Wilsonworks
Art Director: Clare Wilson
Designer: Barry Moyer
Paper/Printing: Three colors on Strathmore Writing Bright White

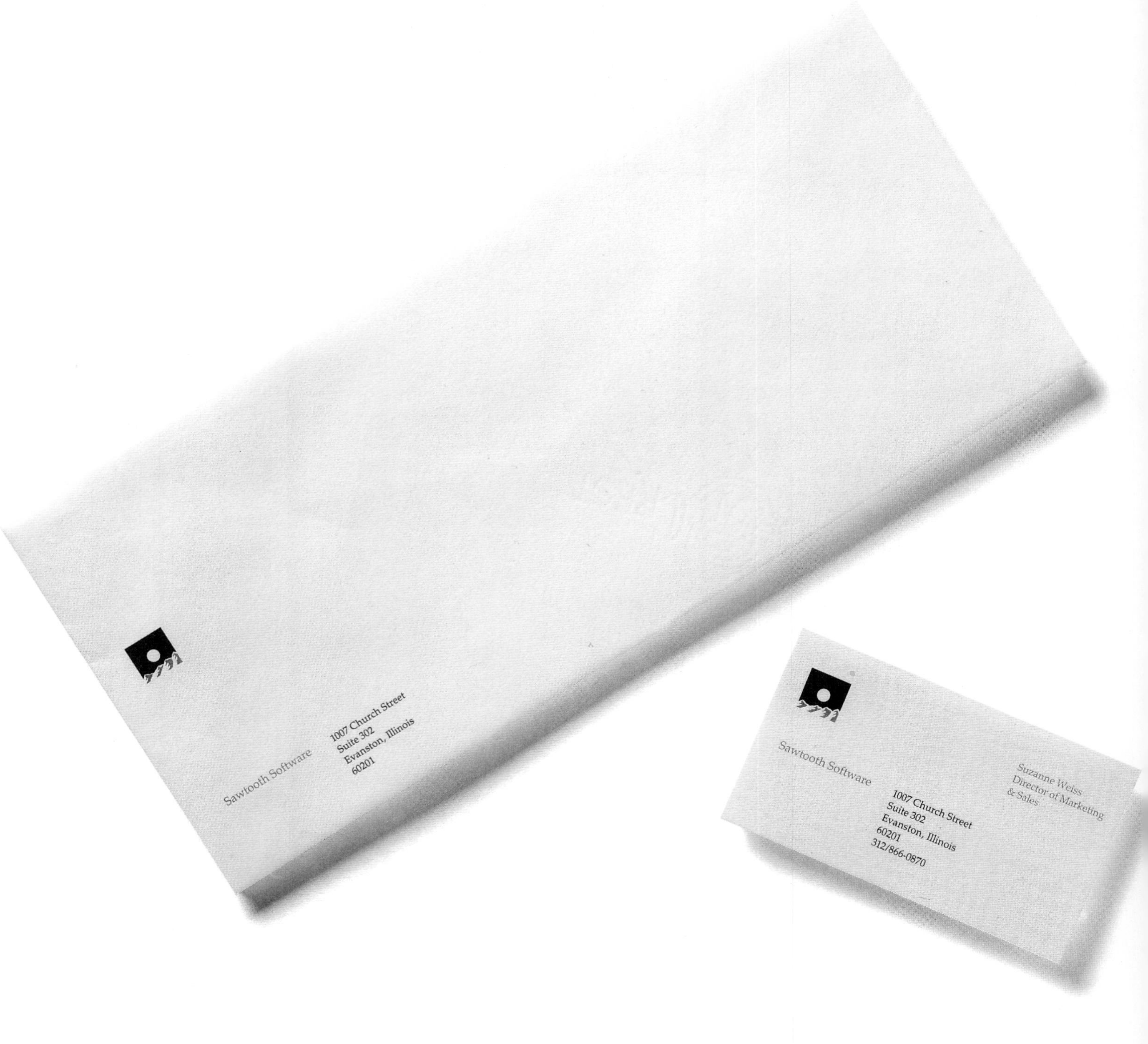

Sawtooth Software

1007 Church Street
Suite 302
Evanston, Illinois
60201

Sawtooth Software

Suzanne Weiss
Director of Marketing
& Sales

1007 Church Street
Suite 302
Evanston, Illinois
60201
312/866-0870

Client: Sawtooth Software
Design Firm: Michael Stanard, Inc.
Art Director: Michael Stanard
Designer: Ann Werner
Paper/Printing: Two colors on Crane's Crest

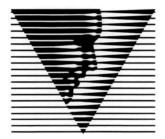

Client: Arch Financial Systems
Design Firm: Design Center
Art Director: John Reger
Designers: Kobe, D.W. Olson

Client: Asymetrix Corporation
Design Firm: Hornall Anderson Design Works
Art Director: Jack Anderson
Designers: Jack Anderson, Julie Tanagi-Lock,
Mary Hermes, Heidi Hatlestad
Illustrator: Brian O'Neill

Client: Rabbit Copier and Service
Design Firm: Tollner Design Group
Art Director: Lisa Tollner
Designer: Karen Saucier
Illustrator: Karen Saucier

Client: Muehling Associates
Design Firm: J. Brelsford Design, Inc.
Art Director: Jerry Brelsford
Designer: Robert Whitmer

Client: Varitronics Systems Inc.
Design Firm: Design Center
Art Director: John Reger
Designer: C.S. Anderson

Client: Bossardt Corporation
Design Firm: Design Center
Art Director: John Reger
Designer: Todd Spichke

Client: Chemical Bank
Design Firm: De Martino Design Inc.
Art Director: Erick De Martino
Designer: Erick De Martino
Illustrator: Erick De Martino

Client: Valid Logic Systems
Design Firm: Tollner Design Group
Art Director: Lisa Tollner
Designer: Kim Tucker
Illustrator: Kim Tucker

Client: Kumar Consulting
Design Firm: Kuo Design Group
Art Director: Samuel Kuo
Designer: Samuel Kuo

Client: Matthew Bender
Design Firm: De Martino Design Inc.
Art Director: Dick Smith
Designer: Erick De Martino
Illustrator: Erick De Martino

Client: Iris System
Design Firm: Michael Stanard, Inc.
Art Director: Michael Stanard
Designer: Ann Werner

Client: Monetary Consultants
Corp.
Design Firm: J. Brelsford Design, Inc.
Art Director: Jerry Brelsford
Designer: Jerry Brelsford

5. GRAPHIC DESIGN / ADVERTISING

Client: Cordella Design
Design Firm: Cordella Design
Art Director: Andreé Cordella
Designer: Andreé Cordella
Paper/Printing: One color and foil

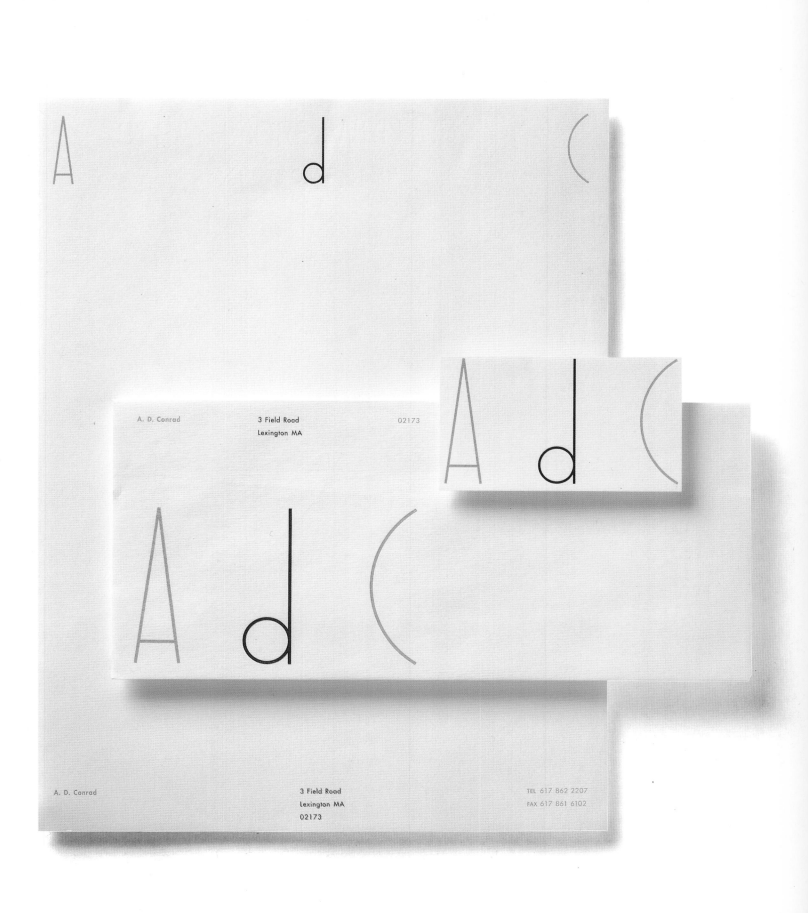

Client: A.d. Conrad
Design Firm: Clifford Selbert Design
Art Director: Clifford Selbert
Designer: Liz Rotter
Typography: Liz Rotter
Paper/Printing: Three colors on Strathmore Writing Bright White Wove

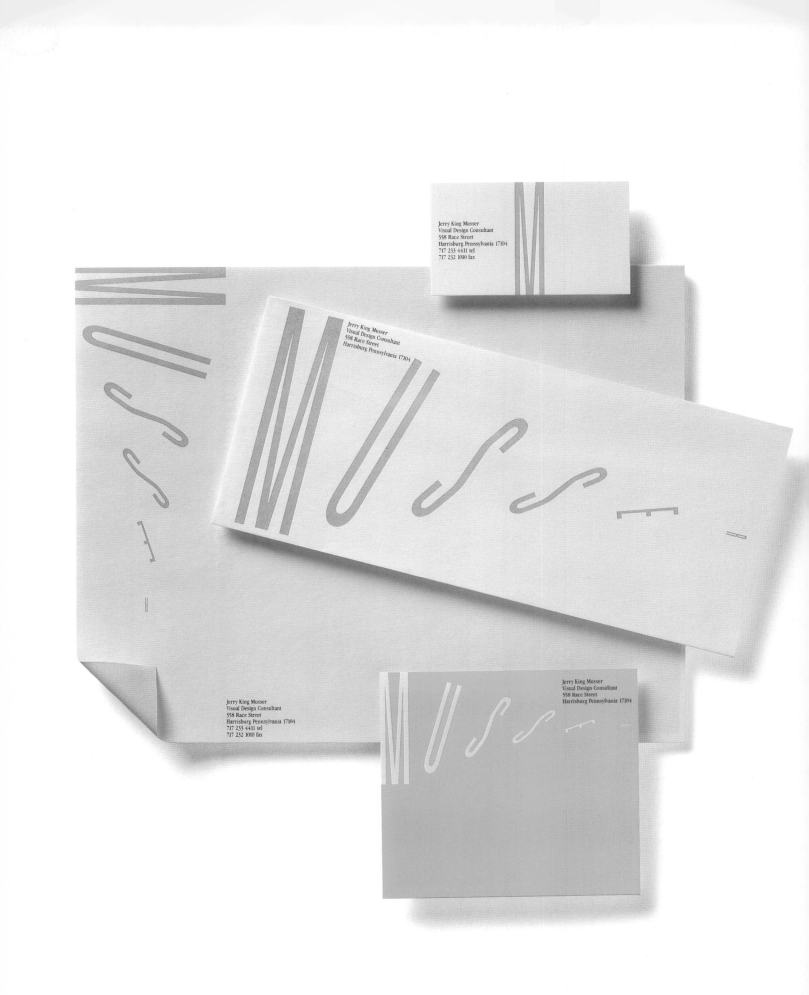

Client: Musser Design
Design Firm: Musser Design
Art Director: Musser
Designer: Musser
Paper/Printing: Two colors on Neenah Bond

REINER *Design Consultants, Inc.*

26 East 22nd. Street, 8th Floor.

New York, NY 10010.

Telephone: 212.673.1302

Fax No. 212.353.2690

REINER *Design Consultants, Inc.*

26 East 22nd. Street

New York, NY 10010.

Telephone: 212.673.1302

Fax No. 212.353.2690

REINER *Design Consultants, Inc.*
26 East 22nd Street
New York, NY 10010
Telephone: 212.673.1302
Fax No. 212.353.2690

Client: Reiner Design Consultants, Inc.
Design Firm: Reiner Design Consultants, Inc.
Art Director: Roger J. Gorman
Designer: Roger J. Gorman
Paper/Printing: Two colors on Strathmore Writing Bright White Wove

Lewin / Holland, Inc.
230 West 17th Street
New York, NY 10011
212 255 6456
Fax 212 989 8494

Lewin / Holland, Inc.
230 West 17th Street
New York, NY 10011

Lewin / Holland, Inc.
230 West 17th Street
New York, NY 10011

Lewin / Holland, Inc.
230 West 17th Street
New York, NY 10011
212 255 6456
Fax 212 989 8494

Marketing & Communications Design

Cheryl Lewin
Principal

Client: Lewin/Holland, Inc.
Design Firm: Lewin/Holland, Inc.
Art Director: Cheryl Lewin
Designer: Cheryl Lewin
Paper/Printing: Two colors

Client: The Dinosaur Group Inc.
Design Firm: The Dinosaur Group Inc.
Art Director: Bill Logan
Designer: Bill Logan
Illustrator: Bill Logan
Paper/Printing: Five colors on Strathmore Writing Grey Laid

Client: Notovitz Design, Inc.
Design Firm: Notovitz Design, Inc.
Art Directors: Joe Notovitz, Gil Livne
Designer: Gil Livne
Paper/Printing: Three colors on Neenah Avon Brilliant White

Client: Marketing By Design
Design Firm: Marketing By Design
Art Director: Joel Stinghen
Designer: Linda Clark Johnson
Illustrator: Linda Clark Johnson
Paper/Printing: Four colors on Clasic Crest

Client: Jack Tom Design
Design Firm: Jack Tom Design
Art Director: Jack Tom
Designer: Jack Tom
Illustrator: Jack Tom
Paper/Printing: Two colors on Gilbert Bond 25% Cotton

Rowe & Ballantine

Rowe & Ballantine

Edward L. Rowe, Jr.

Graphic Design Consultants
P.O. Box 293
8 Galloping Hill Road   Tel: 203-775-7887
Brookfield, CT 06804   Fax: 203-775-7881

Rowe & Ballantine

Rowe & Ballantine

P.O. Box 293
8 Galloping Hill Road
Brookfield, CT 06804

P.O. Box 293
8 Galloping Hill Road
Brookfield, CT 06804

Rowe & Ballantine   P.O. Box 293   Tel: 203-775-7887
Graphic Design Consultants   8 Galloping Hill Road   Fax: 203-775-7881
Brookfield, CT 06804

Client:	Rowe & Ballantine
Design Firm:	Rowe & Ballantine
Art Director:	Edward L. Rowe, Jr.
Designer:	John H. Ballantine
Paper/Printing:	Two colors on Strathmore Writing

GROH

Carol Groh & Associates

Carol Groh & Associates
645 Madison Avenue
New York, New York 10022

Interior Planning/
Design/Graphics

Jill Hammerberg

Carol Groh & Associates
645 Madison Avenue
New York, New York 10022

Tel: 212.935.2900
Fax: 212.826.6926

Interior Planning/Design/Graphics

645 Madison Avenue
New York, New York 10022

Interior Planning/
Design/Graphics

Carol Groh & Associates

645 Madison Avenue
New York, New York 10022

Tel: 212.935.2900
Fax: 212.826.6926

Interior Planning/
Design/Graphics

Client: Carol Groh & Associates
Design Firm: Donovan and Green
Art Director: Nancye Green
Designer: Clint Morgan
Paper/Printing: Six colors on Protocol 100 Warm White Wove

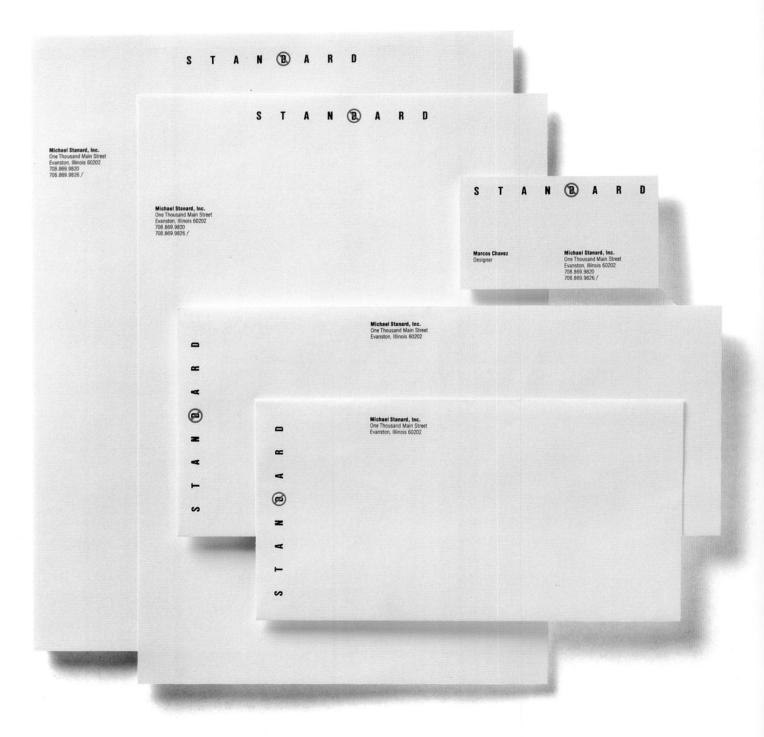

Client: Michael Standard, Inc.
Design Firm: Michael Stanard
Art Director: Michael Stanard
Designer: Michael Stanard
Paper/Printing: Two colors on Strathmore Writing

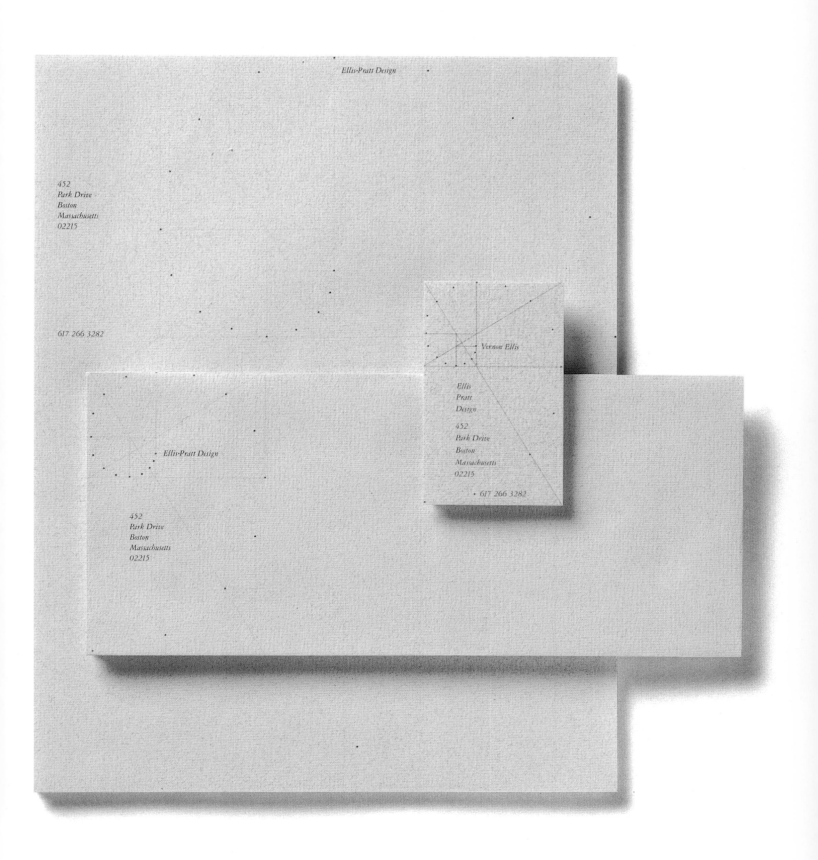

Client: Ellis • Pratt Design
Design Firm: Ellis • Pratt Design
Art Directors: Vernon Ellis, Elaine Pratt
Designers: Elaine Pratt, Vernon Ellis
Paper/Printing: Two colors on Simpson Gainsborough

Client: I Pezzi Dipinti
Design Firm: M Plus M Incorporated
Art Directors: Takaaki Matsumoto, Michael McGinn
Designer: Takaaki Matsumoto

Client: Margo Chase Design
Design Firm: Margo Chase Design
Art Director: Margo Chase
Designer: Margo Chase
Paper/Printing: Three colors on Mountie Matte White

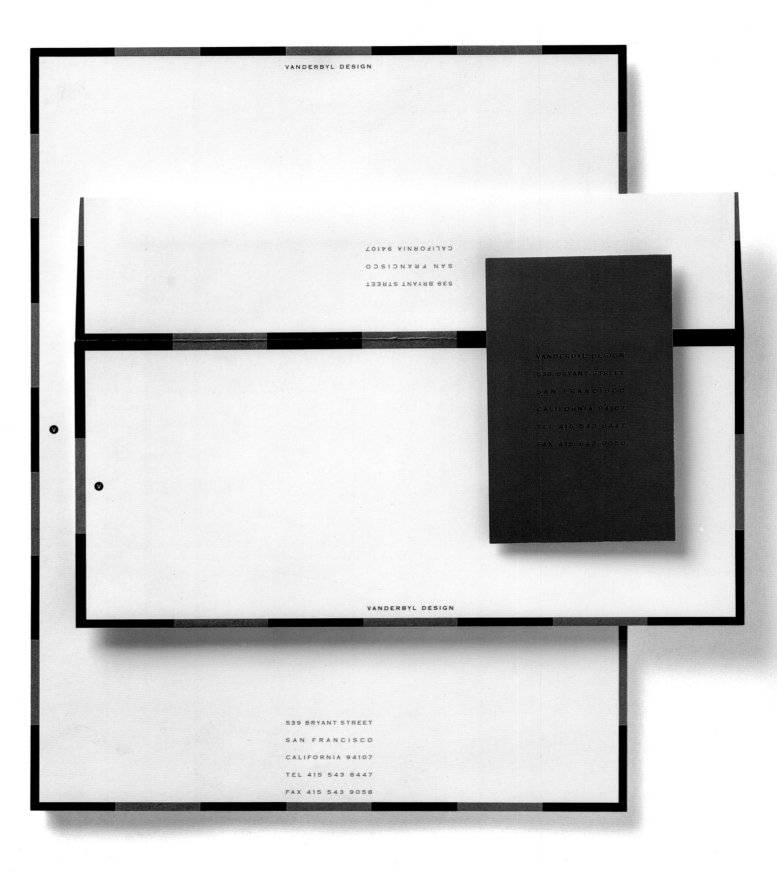

Client: Vanderbyl Design
Design Firm: Vanderbyl Design
Designer: Michael Vanderbyl
Paper/Printing: Two colors on Starwhite Vicksburg

Client:	James Strange
Design Firm:	Culver & Associates
Art Director:	James Strange
Designer:	James Strange
Illustrator:	James Strange
Paper/Printing:	One color on Speckletone Chalk White

Client:	Adam, Filippo & Associates
Design Firm:	Adam, Filippo & Associates
Art Directors:	Robert Adam, Louis Filippo
Designer:	Barbara S. Peak
Paper/Printing:	Two colors and blind embossing on Strathmore Writing Ultimate White Laid Finish

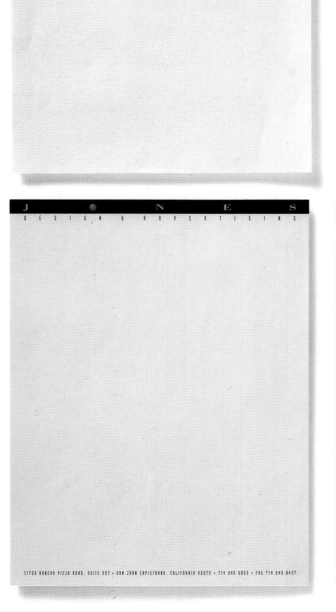

Client:	Jones Design & Advertising
Design Firm:	Jones Design & Advertising
Art Director:	Scott Marsh
Designer:	Scott Marsh
Illustrator:	Melissa Latham-Stevens
Paper/Printing:	Three colors on EverGreen Script

Client:	Robert Cook Design
Design Firm:	Robert Cook Design
Art Director:	Robert Cook
Designer:	Robert Cook
Paper/Printing:	Four colors on Strathmore Writing

Client: Clark Keller, Inc.
Design Firm: Clark Keller, Inc.
Art Director: Jane Keller
Designer: Neal M. Ashby
Paper/Printing: Six colors on Eloquence Strathmore Bond

Client: Design Office of Emery/Poe
Design Firm: Emery/Poe Design
Art Director: David Poe
Designer: David Poe
Paper/Printing: Three colors on Zanders

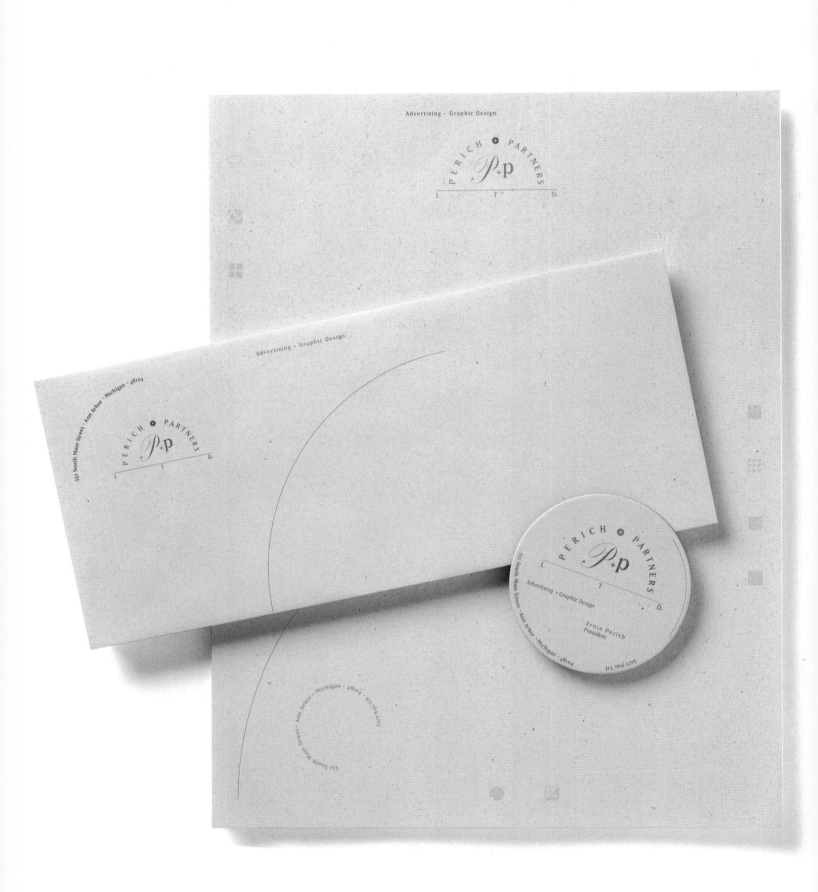

Client: Perich + Partners
Design Firm: Perich + Partners
Art Director: Ernie Perich
Designers: Carol Mooradian, Scott Pryor
Paper/Printing: Four colors on Neenah Environment

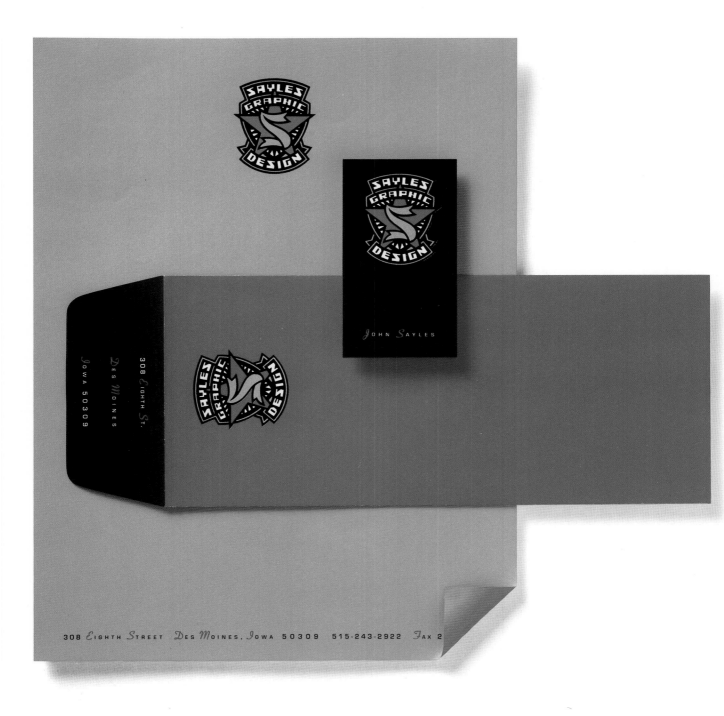

Client: Sayles Graphic Design
Design Firm: Sayles Graphic Design
Art Director: John Sayles
Designer: John Sayles
Paper/Printing: Three colors and foil on Neenah Classic Crest

Client: Manhattan Design
Design Firm: Manhattan Design
Designer: Frank Olinsky
Illustrator: Frank Olinsky
Paper/Printing: Two colors

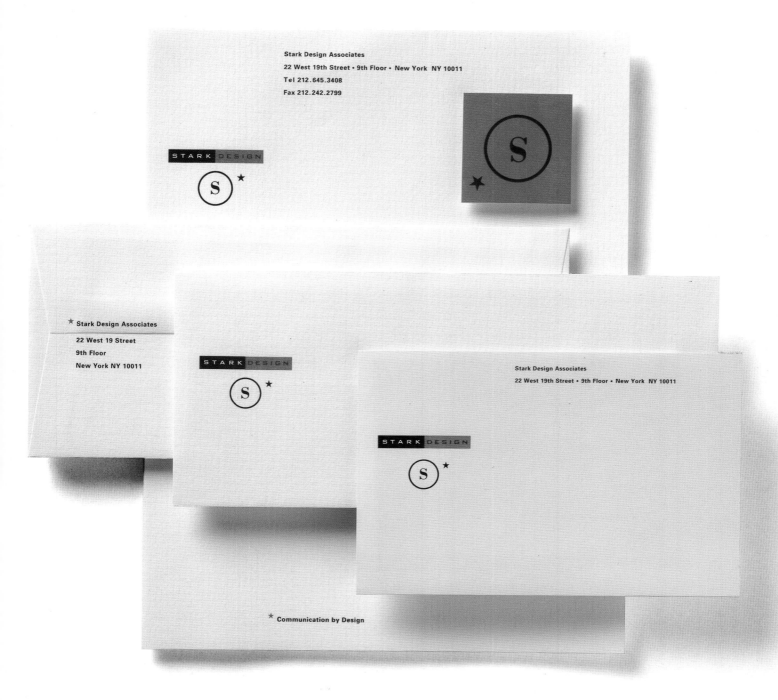

Client: Stark Design Associates
Design Firm: Stark Design Associates
Art Director: Adriane Stark
Designer: Adriane Stark
Paper/Printing: Two colors on Gilbert Esse

Client: Rick Eiber Design (RED)
Design Firm: Rick Eiber Design
Art Director: Rick Eiber
Designer: Rick Eiber
Paper/Printing: Four colors on Starwhite Vicksburg Vellum

Client: Qually & Company Inc.
Design Firm: Qually & Company Inc.
Art Director: Robert Qually
Designer: Robert Qually
Illustrator: Alex Murawski
Paper/Printing: Four colors on Mead

Client: De Martino Design Inc.
Design Firm: De Martino Design Inc.
Art Director: Erick De Martino
Designer: Carol Maisto
Illustrator: Carol Maisto
Paper/Printing: Two colors on Strathmore Writing Bright White

Qually & Company, Inc

Advertising/Design/Product Development

30 E. Huron-Suite 2502

Chicago, Illinois 60611, U.S.A

By phone: (312) 944-0237

DEMARTINO
DESIGN▲INC

5 6 4
BROADWAY
•
NEW YORK
NEW YORK
•
1 0 0 1 2

2 1 2
941-9200

HAFEMAN DESIGN GROUP

935 West Chestnut, Suite 203

Chicago, Illinois 60622

Telephone 312 829.6829

Facsimile 312 829.6697

GUNNAR SWANSON DESIGN OFFICE

739 INDIANA AVENUE

VENICE, CALIFORNIA 90291-2728

310/399-5191

FAX: 310/399-2675

Client: Hafeman Design Group
Design Firm: Hafeman Design Group
Art Director: William Hafeman
Designers: William Hafeman, Gabrielle Schubart
Paper/Printing: Two colors on Gilbert Neu-Tech

Client: Gunnar Swanson Design Office
Design Firm: Gunnar Swanson Design Office
Art Director: Gunnar Swanson
Designer: Gunnar Swanson
Paper/Printing: Letterhead - Three colors on Curtis Parchkin Riblaid,
Envelopes - Simpson Evergreen,
Business Card - Regal PCW

Janell Genovese

328 Washington St

Somerville, MA

02143 776-7047

Graphic Design

Client: Janell Genovese
Design Firm: Janell Genovese Design
Art Director: Janell Genovese
Designer: Janell Genovese
Paper/Printing: Two colors and varnish on Strathmore White Wove Groove

sequel.

sequel, incorporated
310 west liberty street
suite 300
louisville, kentucky 40202
502 . 583 . 5132
502 . 569 . 7211 fax

phillip h. means
director of graphic design

graphic design
corporate communications

sequel.

sequel.

Sequel, Inc.

732 West Main Street

Louisville, Kentucky 40202

502 . 583 . 5132

502 . 569 . 7211 fax

Graphic Design
Corporate Communications

graphic design
corporate communications

sequel.

sequel, incorporated
310 west liberty street
suite 300
louisville, kentucky 40202

graphic design
corporate communications

Client: Sequel, Inc.
Design Firm: Sequel, Inc.
Art Directors: Denise Olding, Phil Means
Designer: Denise Olding
Paper/Printing: Two colors on Curtis Brightwater Writing Riblaid

Client: Traver & Associates
Design Firm: Traver & Associates
Art Director: Stephen Thompson
Designer: Stephen Thompson
Paper/Printing: Two colors on French Rayon

Client: Advertising Professionals of Des Moines
Design Firm: Sayles Graphic Design
Art Director: John Sayles
Designer: John Sayles
Paper/Printing: Two colors on James River Tuscan Terra

Client: Tharp Did It
Design Firm: Tharp Did It • Los Gatos/San Francisco
Art Director: Rick Tharp
Designers: Rick Tharp, Karen Nomura, Jana Heer, Jean Mogannam
Paper/Printing: Two colors, foil, and embossing on Crane's Crest and Simpson Starwhite Vicksburg

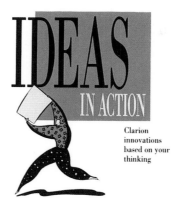

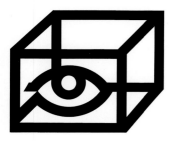

Client: Clarion Marketing and
Communications
Design Firm: Clarion Marketing and
Communications
Art Director: Kurt Gibson
Designer: Kurt Gibson
Illustrator: Linda Bleck

Client: Insite Design Inc.
Design Firm: De Martino Design Inc.
Art Director: Erick De Martino
Designer: Erick De Martino
Illustrator: Erick De Martino

Client: Unlimited Swan, Inc.
Design Firm: Unlimited Swan, Inc.
Art Director: Jim Swan
Designer: Jim Swan
Illustrator: Jim Swan

Client: Kuo Design Group
Design Firm: Kuo Design Group
Art Director: Samuel Kuo
Designer: Samuel Kuo

PHOTOGRAPHY

Client: Roger Lee Studio
Design Firm: Vanderbyl Design
Designer: Michael Vanderbyl
Paper/Printing: Two colors on Starwhite Vicksburg

Client: Patrick Fox Photography
Design Firm: William Homan Design
Art Director: William Homan
Designer: William Homan
Paper/Printing: Two colors

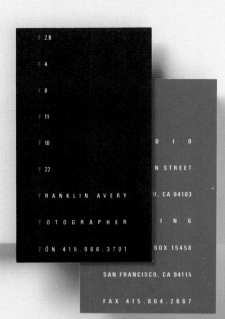

F 2.8

F 4

F 8

F 11

F 16

F 22

FRANKLIN AVERY

FOTOGRAPHER

FŌN 415.986.3701

POST OFFICE BOX 15458

SAN FRANCISCO, CA 94115

POST OFFICE BOX 15458, SAN FRANCISCO, CALIFORNIA 94115

FROM   FRANKLIN AVERY

FOR

Client: Franklin Avery
Design Firm: Tharp Did It • Los Gatos/San Francisco
Art Director: Rick Tharp
Designers: Kim Tomlinson, Rick Tharp
Paper/Printing: Two colors on Simpson Starwhite Vicksburg

Client: Joseph Dieter Visual Communications
Design Firm: Joseph Dieter Visual Communications
Art Director: Joseph M. Dieter, Jr.
Designer: Joseph M. Dieter, Jr.
Paper/Printing: Two colors on Strathmore Writing

CHRIS CALLIS STUDIO INC.

Client: Chris Callis
Design Firm: M & Co.
Designers: Emily Oberman, Tibor Kalman

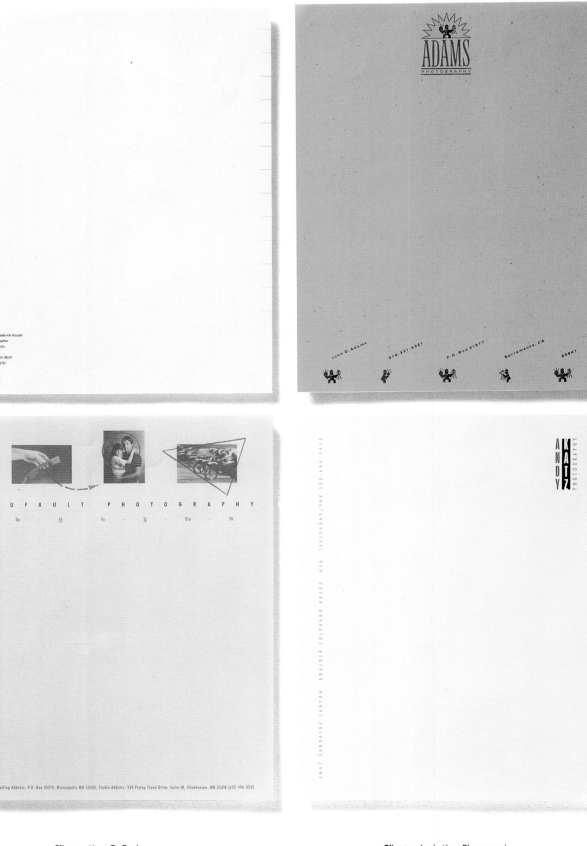

Client: James Frederick Housel
Design Firm: Hornall Anderson Design Works
Art Director: Jack Anderson
Designers: Jack Anderson, Raymond Terada
Paper/Printing: Eight colors on Strathmore Writing

Client: Adams Photography
Art Director: Laurel Bigley
Designer: Laurel Bigley
Illustrator: Laurel Bigley
Paper/Printing: Letterhead - Three colors on Evergreen Kraft,
Envelopes - Wausau Vellum Opaque

Client: Kent DuFault
Design Firm: Steve Lundgren Graphic Design
Art Director: Steve Lundgren
Designer: Steve Lundgren
Illustrator: Steve Lundgren
Paper/Printing: Two colors on Neenah Classic Crest

Client: Andy Katz Photography
Design Firm: Communication Arts Inc.
Art Director: Richard Foy
Designer: Hugh Enockson

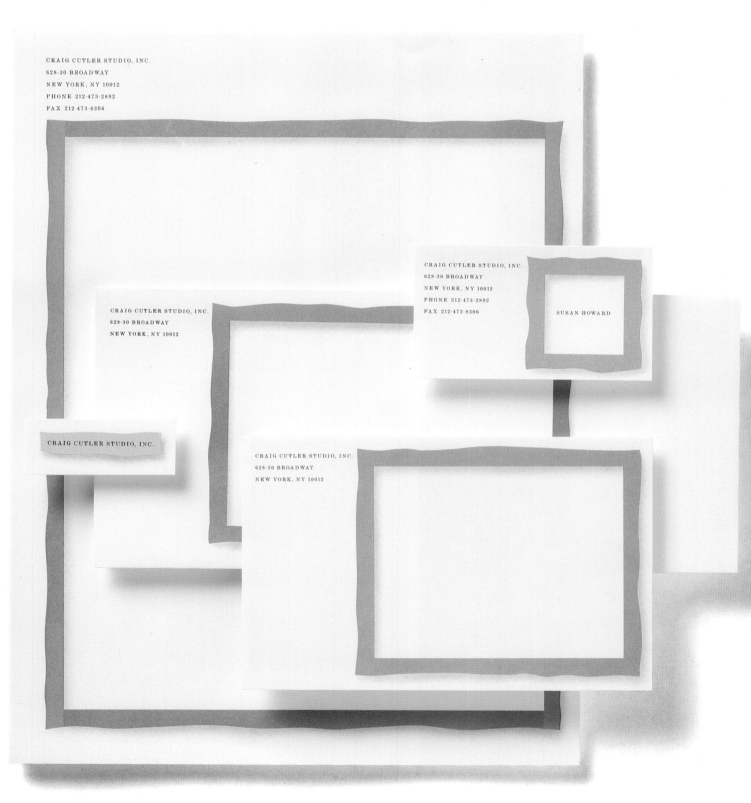

Client: Craig Cutler Studio, Inc.
Design Firm: The Pushpin Group
Designer: Greg Simpson

Client: City Light Studio
Design Firm: Urban Taylor & Associates
Art Director: Alan Urban
Designer: Alan Urban
Illustrator: Alan Urban
Paper/Printing: Four color process on Consolidated Frostbite

Client: Smashbox
Design Firm: Margo Chase Design
Art Director: Margo Chase
Designer: Margo Chase
Paper/Printing: Two colors and foil on Speckletone Chipboard

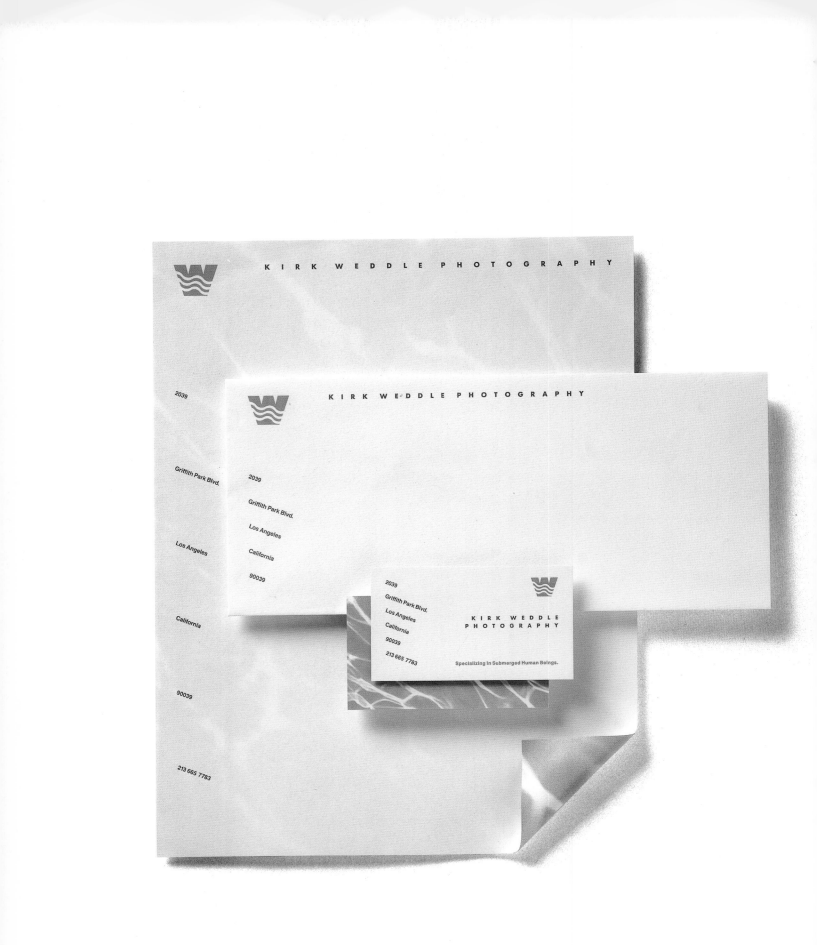

Client: Kirk Weddle Photography
Design Firm: Tracy Mac Design
Art Director: Tracy McGoldrick
Designer: Tracy McGoldrick
Paper/Printing: Two colors on Crane's Crest

Client: Axiom, Inc.
Design Firm: McCord Graphic Design
Art Director: Walter McCord
Designer: Walter McCord
Illustrator: Walter McCord
Paper/Printing: Two colors on Simpson Protocol

7. ARCHITECTS

Client: Station 19
Design Firm: Design Center
Art Director: John Reger
Designer: Kobe
Paper/Printing: Four colors

D'AGOSTINO IZZO QUIRK ARCHITECTS
432 COLUMBIA STREET   CAMBRIDGE, MA 02141   TELEPHONE 617 547 3935   FAX 617 547 0990

Client: DAIQ Architects
Design Firm: Communication Arts, Inc.
Art Director: Richard Foy
Designer: David A. Shelton
Paper/Printing: Two colors on Strathmore Writing White Laid

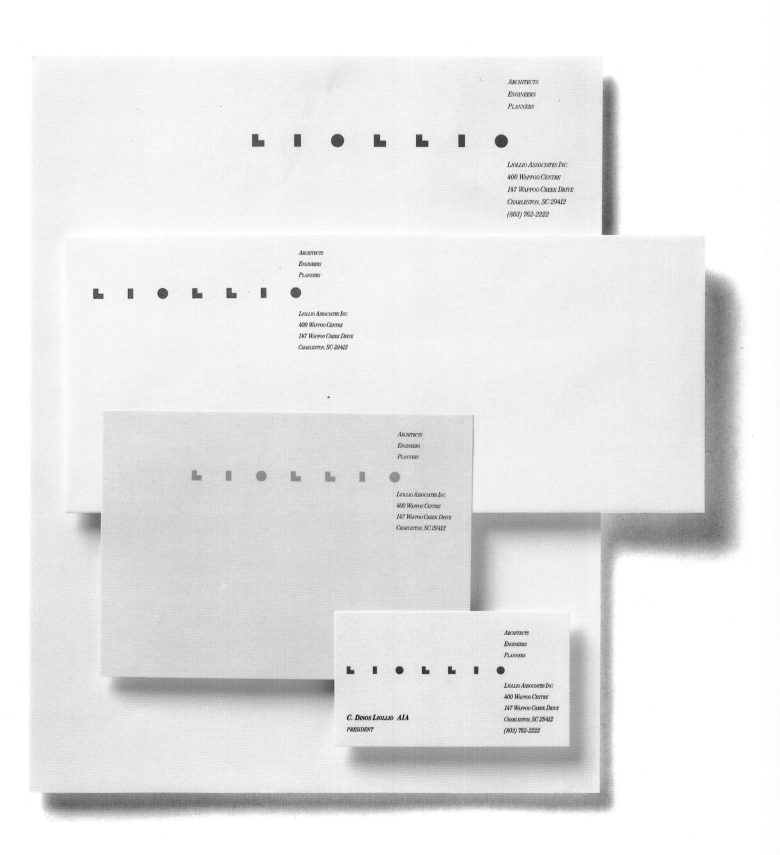

Client: Liollio Associates
Design Firm: Rousso+Associates, Inc.
Art Director: Steve Rousso
Designer: Steve Rousso
Paper/Printing: Two colors on Strathmore Writing

Client: CYP, Inc.
Design Firm: Davies Associates
Art Director: Noel Davies
Designers: Meredith Kamm, Cathy Tetef
Paper/Printing: Two colors and clear foil on Gilbert Neu-Tech Kromekote

Client: Lineage Homes
Design Firm: Puccinelli Design
Art Director: Keith Puccinelli
Designer: Keith Puccinelli
Illustrator: Keith Puccinelli
Paper/Printing: Four colors on Strathmore Writing

Client: Rojas•Vogt Associates Inc.
Design Firm: Kevin P. Sheehan Design
Art Director: Kevin Sheehan
Designer: Kevin Sheehan
Paper/Printing: Two colors on Curtis Brightwater

Client: Snyder Wick Associates
Design Firm: Michael Stanard Inc.
Art Director: Michael Stanard
Designers: Michael Stanard, Marcos Chavez
Paper/Printing: Two colors on Strathmore Writing

INTĚGRUS
ARCHITECTURE

WEST 244 MAIN AVENUE
SPOKANE, WA 99201
P.O. BOX 1482 (99210)

FAX 509.838.2194
509.838.8681

INTĚGRUS
ARCHITECTURE

915 SEATTLE TOWER
1218 THIRD AVENUE
SEATTLE, WA 98101-3018

The WMFL & ECI traditions continue.

INTĚGRUS
ARCHITECTURE

The WMFL & ECI traditions continue.

INTĚGRUS
ARCHITECTURE

JOHN PLIMLEY, P.E.
STRUCTURAL ENGINEER, PRINCIPAL

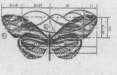

WEST 244 MAIN AVENUE
SPOKANE, WA 99201
P.O. BOX 1482 (99210)

FAX 509.838.2194
509.838.8681

The WMFL & ECI traditions continue.

Larry D. Hurlbert
William A. James
Gary D. Joralemon
Bruce F. Mauser
George H. Nachtsheim
Arthur A. Nordling
John Plimley
Gordon E. Ruehl
Thomas M. Shine
Bruce M. Walker
Gerald A. Winkler
Kirklund S. Wise

The WMFL & ECI traditions continue.

Client: Integrus
Design Firm: Hornall Anderson Design Works
Art Director: John Hornall
Designers: John Hornall, Paula Cox, Brian O'Neill
Paper/Printing: Two colors on Neenah Environment

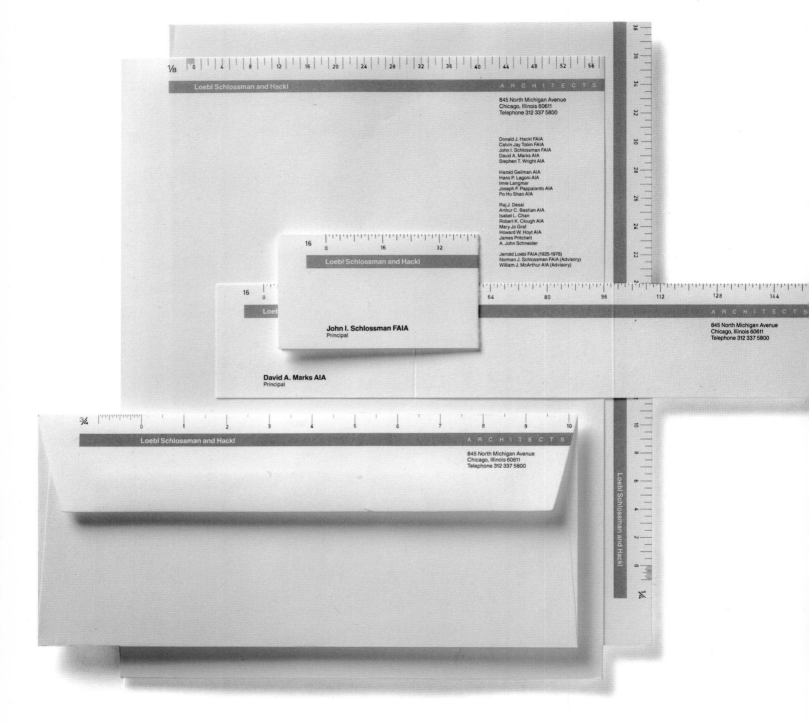

Client: Loebl Schlossman & Hackl
Design Firm: Rick Eiber Design (RED)
Art Director: Rick Eiber
Designer: Rick Eiber
Paper/Printing: Two colors on Classic Crest

Client: Nixon Johnson Architectural Associates
Design Firm: Pollman Marketing Arts, Inc.
Art Director: Jennifer Pollman
Designer: Jennifer Pollman
Paper/Printing: Two colors on Tiara High-tech 80# text Vicksburg

SILBERSTANG ARCHITECTS PC

19 West 21st Street

New York NY 10010

212 242 3234

SILBERSTANG ARCHITECTS PC

19 West 21st Street

New York NY 10010

SILBERSTANG ARCHITECTS PC

19 West 21st Street

New York NY 10010

212 242 3234

Alan Barry Silberstang   AIA NCARB

Client: Silberstang Architects
Design Firm: Barry David Berger + Associates, Inc.
Art Director: Barry Berger
Designer: Heidi Broecking
Paper/Printing: One color

ARCHITECTS
COLLINS·HANSEN

Michael P. Collins

COLLINS·HANSEN

ARCHITECTS

Suite 305
126 Third Street North
Minneapolis, MN 55401
612·338·8181

Suite 305, 126 Third Street North, Minneapolis, MN 55401

ARCHITECTS
COLLINS·HANSEN

Suite 305, 126 Third Street North
Minneapolis, MN 55401

COLLINS·HANSEN

ARCHITECTS

Suite 305, 126 Third Street North, Minneapolis, MN 55401 612·338·8181

Client: Collins-Hansen Architects
Design Firm: Steve Lundgren Graphic Design
Art Director: Steve Lundgren
Designer: Steve Lundgren
Illustrator: Steve Lundgren
Paper/Printing: Two colors on Simpson Protocol 100

8. MASS MEDIA

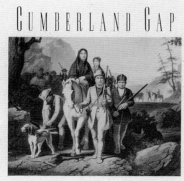

CUMBERLAND GAP

PRODUCTIONS

CUMBERLAND GAP

PRODUCTIONS

CUMBERLAND GAP

PRODUCTIONS

ELEANOR BINGHAM MILLER

635 WEST MAIN STREET

THIRD FLOOR

LOUISVILLE, KENTUCKY 40202

(502) 587-7348

635 WEST MAIN STREET THIRD FLOOR LOUISVILLE, KENTUCKY 40202 (502) 587-7348

Client: Cumberland Gap
Design Firm: McCord Graphic Design
Art Directors: Walter McCord, Eleanor Miller
Designer: Walter McCord
Illustrator: George Caleb Bingham
Paper/Printing: Four colors on Simpson EverGreen Birch

Client: Video Jukebox Network Inc.
Design Firm: Urban Taylor & Associates
Art Director: Alan Urban
Designer: Alan Urban
Paper/Printing: Three colors on Simpson Starwhite Vicksburg

KXXX-FM
530 BUSH STREET
SAN FRANCISCO, CA 94108
415.951.7200
FAX 415.951.7279

X·100

CAREY CHAN
Programming Assistant

X·100

KXXX-FM
530 BUSH STREET
SAN FRANCISCO, CA 94108
415.951.7200
FAX 415.951.7279

KXXX-FM
530 BUSH STREET
SAN FRANCISCO, CA 94108

X·100

AN EMMIS BROADCASTING STATION

Client: Emmis Broadcasting Corporation
Design Firm: Tharp Did It • Los Gatos/San Francisco
Art Director: Rick Tharp
Designers: Rick Tharp, Kim Tomlinson
Paper/Printing: Three colors and embossing on Simpson Starwhite Vicksburg

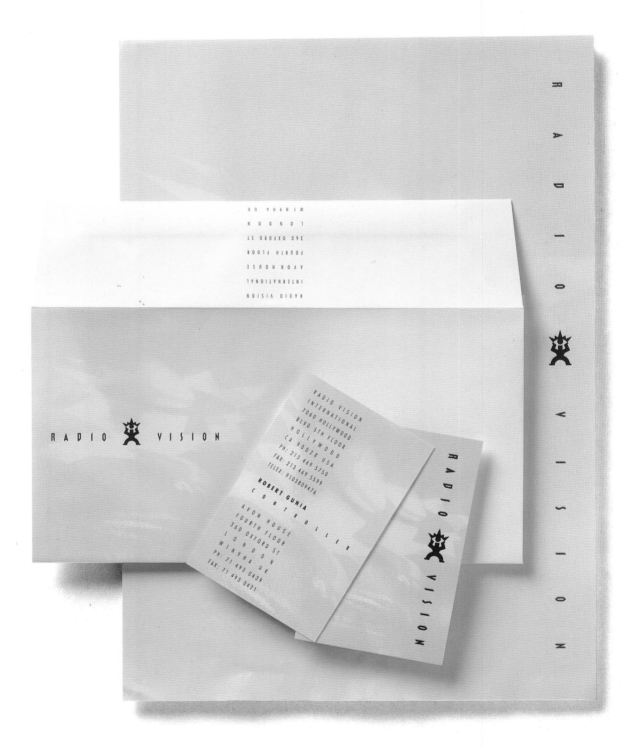

Client: Radio Vision International
Design Firm: Margo Chase Design
Art Director: Margo Chase
Designer: Margo Chase
Paper/Printing: Three colors on Mountie Matte White

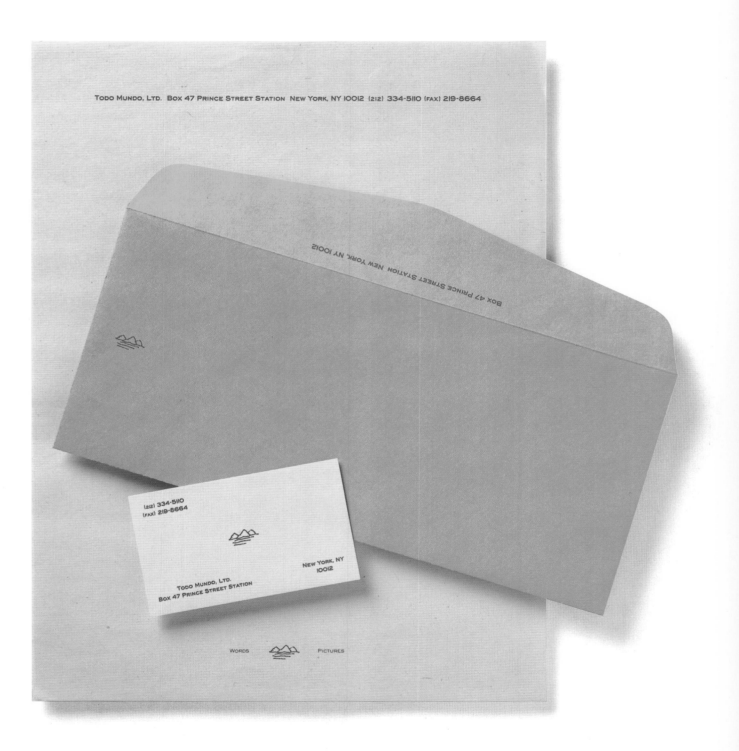

Client: Todo Mundo
Design Firm: M & Co.
Designers: Tibor Kalman, Emily Oberman
Illustrator: Maira Kalman

Client: Inside Productions
Design Firm: Unlimited Swan, Inc.
Art Director: Jim Swan
Designer: Jim Swan
Illustrator: Jim Swan
Paper/Printing: Three colors on Strathmore Writing

Client: New York Television Inc.
Design Firm: Katz Wheeler Design
Art Director: Alina R. Wheeler
Designer: Jody Marx
Paper/Printing: Two colors on Strathmore Writing

Client: Pulse Of The Planet
Design Firm: Louise Fili Ltd.
Art Director: Louise Fili
Designer: Louise Fili
Illustrator: Anthony Russo
Paper/Printing: Two colors on Strathmore Writing

Client: Newbury Film Works
Design Firm: Marc English: Design
Art Director: Marc English
Designer: Marc English
Paper/Printing: Three colors on French Speckletone

Client: Houston Winn Films
Design Firm: Unlimited Swan, Inc.
Art Director: Jim Swan
Designer: Jim Swan
Illustrator: Jim Swan
Paper/Printing: Three colors and clear foil stamp

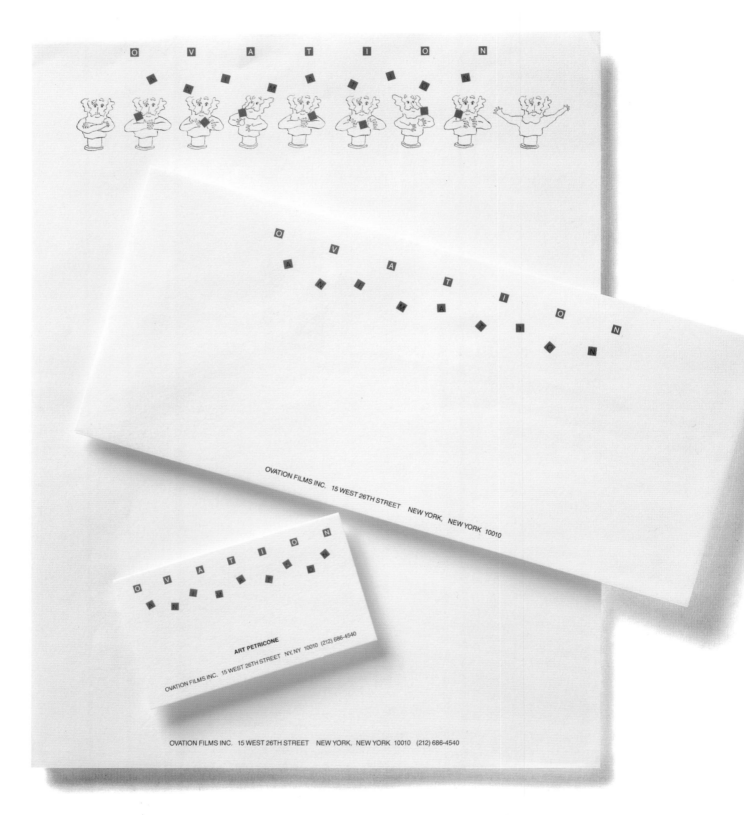

Client: Ovation Animation
Design Firm: Frank D'Astolfo Design
Art Director: Frank D'Astolfo
Designer: Frank D'Astolfo
Paper/Printing: Two colors on Strathmore Writing

Client: Linda Emery Producer
Design Firm: Emery/Poe Design
Art Director: David Poe
Designer: David Poe
Illustrator: David Poe
Paper/Printing: Four colors on Strathmore Writing

Client: Christopher Howard
Design Firm: Margo Chase Design
Art Director: Margo Chase
Designer: Margo Chase
Paper/Printing: Three colors on Vellum

CELESTIAL FILMS

200 BULKLEY
SAUSALITO
CA. 94965
TEL 415.331.7705
FAX 415.331.4532

Client: Celestial Films
Design Firm: Vanderbyl Design
Designer: Michael Vanderbyl
Paper/Printing: Karma

Client: Pangaea Records
Design Firm: Manhattan Design
Designers: Pat Gorman, Frank Olinsky
Paper/Printing: Three colors

HB&B PRODUCTIONS, INC.
219 EAST 49TH STREET
NEW YORK CITY 10017

DAVID BUSKIN

HB&B PRODUCTIONS, INC.
219 EAST 49TH STREET
NEW YORK CITY 10017
PHONE: 212 758 4120
FAX: 212 758 7304

HB&B PRODUCTIONS, INC.
219 EAST 49TH STREET
NEW YORK CITY 10017
PHONE: 212 758 4120
FAX: 212 758 7304

Client: HB&B
Design Firm: Unlimited Swan, Inc.
Art Director: Jim Swan
Designer: Jim Swan
Illustrator: Jim Swan
Paper/Printing: Three colors on Strathmore Writing

Client: Film Fox
Design Firm: Ashby Design
Art Director: Neal M. Ashby
Designer: Neal M. Ashby
Paper/Printing: One color on Kraft Speckletone

Client: Unicorn Studios
Design Firm: LeeAnn Brook Design
Art Director: LeeAnn Brook
Designer: LeeAnn Brook
Paper/Printing: Two colors on Gilcrest Laid

Client: XYZ Productions
Design Firm: Frank D'Astolfo Design
Art Director: Frank D'Astolfo
Designer: Frank D'Astolfo
Paper/Printing: Three colors on Strathmore Writing

Client: Cotts Films
Design Firm: Unlimited Swan, Inc.
Art Director: Jim Swan
Designer: Jim Swan
Illustrator: Jim Swan
Paper/Printing: Two colors on Strathmore Bond

...eek ☐ Office of the Publisher ☐ 1221 Avenue of the Americas ☐ New York, N.Y. 10020

Client: Business Week Magazine
Design Firm: Design Center
Art Director: John Reger
Designers: D.W. Olson, Kobe
Paper/Printing: Two colors

BusinessWeek

Office of the Publisher

1221 Avenue of the Americas

New York, N.Y. 10020

Client: Business Week Magazine
Design Firm: Design Center
Art Director: John Reger
Designer: D.W. Olson

9. CREATIVE SERVICES

MARSHA FOGEL

*CONTEMPORARY
ART CONSULTANT*

MARSHA FOGEL

*CONTEMPORARY
ART CONSULTANT*

MARSHA FOGEL

*CONTEMPORARY
ART CONSULTANT*

101 CENTRAL PARK WEST NEW YORK NY 10023 TEL 212 724-4132

101 CENTRAL PARK WEST NEW YORK NY 10023

101 CENTRAL PARK WEST NEW YORK NY 10023 TELEPHONE 212 724-4132

Client: Marsha Fogel
Design Firm: Anthony McCall Associates
Art Director: Anthony McCall
Designer: Wing Chan
Paper/Printing: Two colors on Strathmore Ultimate White

Client: Artfact
Design Firm: Thomas Nielsen Design
Art Director: Thomas Nielsen
Designer: Thomas Nielsen
Paper/Printing: Two colors on Poseidon Perfect White

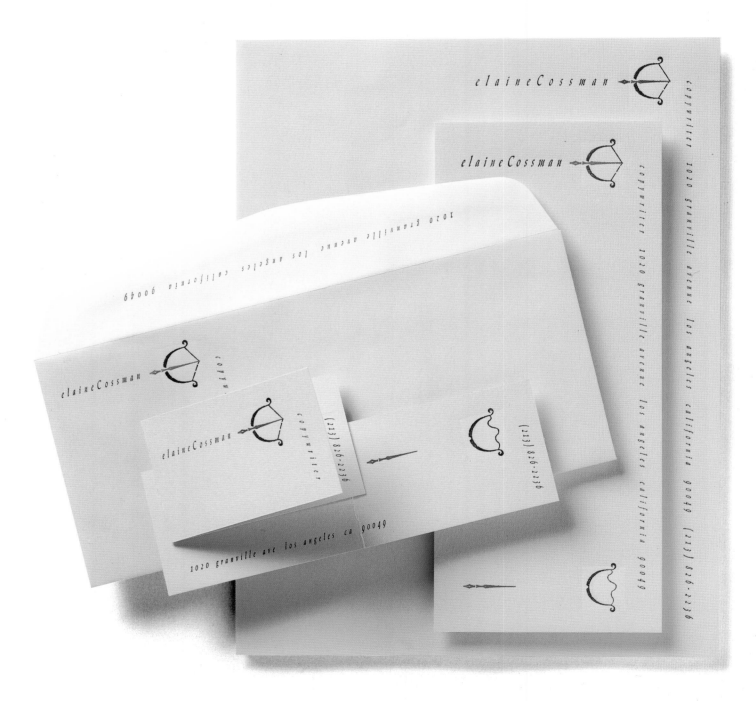

Client: Elaine Cossman
Design Firm: Margo Chase Design
Art Director: Margo Chase
Designer: Margo Chase
Paper/Printing: Three colors on Simpson Protocol

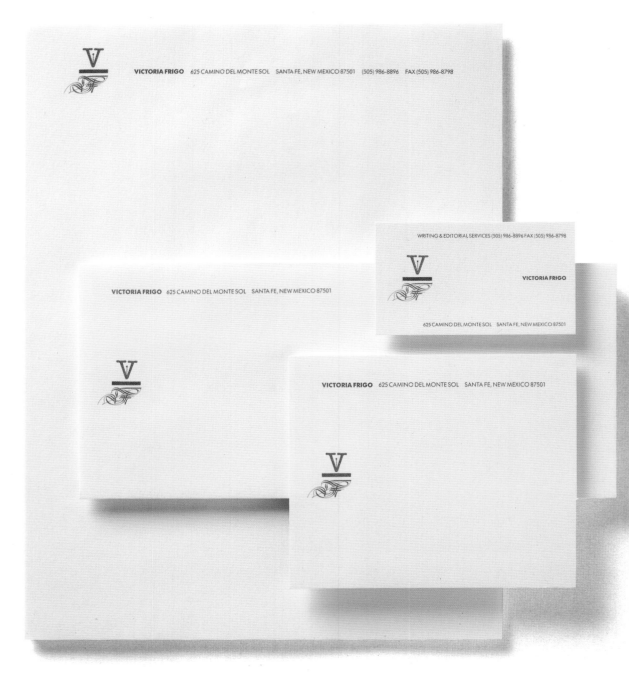

Client: Victoria Frigo
Design Firm: Porter/Matjasich & Associates
Art Director: Allen Porter
Designer: Robert Rausch
Illustrator: Robert Rausch
Paper/Printing: Two colors on Strathmore Writing

Client: El Dorado Ranch
Design Firm: Lawrence Bender & Associates
Art Director: Lawrence Bender
Designer: Margaret Hellmann
Illustrator: Margaret Hellmann
Paper/Printing: Two colors on Neenah Classic Crest Dorian Grey

Client: Arts & Interiors
Design Firm: Douglas + Voss Group
Paper/Printing: Three colors on Curtis Brightwater Writing

Client: The Copy-Cats
Design Firm: J.T. Taverna Associates, Inc.
Designer: Tom Taverna
Paper/Printing: Two colors on Strathmore Writing

Client: Glassworks
Design Firm: Hornall Anderson Design Works
Art Director: Jack Anderson
Designers: Jack Anderson, David Bates
Illustrator/Calligrapher: Tim Girvin
Paper/Printing: Two colors on Starwhite Vicksburg

Client: Persephone Enterprises, Ltd.
Design Firm: Reiner Design Consultants, Inc.
Art Director: Roger J. Gorman
Designer: Roger J. Gorman
Paper/Printing: Three colors on Strathmore Writing Bright White Wove

Client: The Laserworks
Design Firm: Hornall Anderson Design Works
Art Director: Jack Anderson
Designers: Jack Anderson, Cliff Chung
Paper/Printing: Two colors on Strathmore

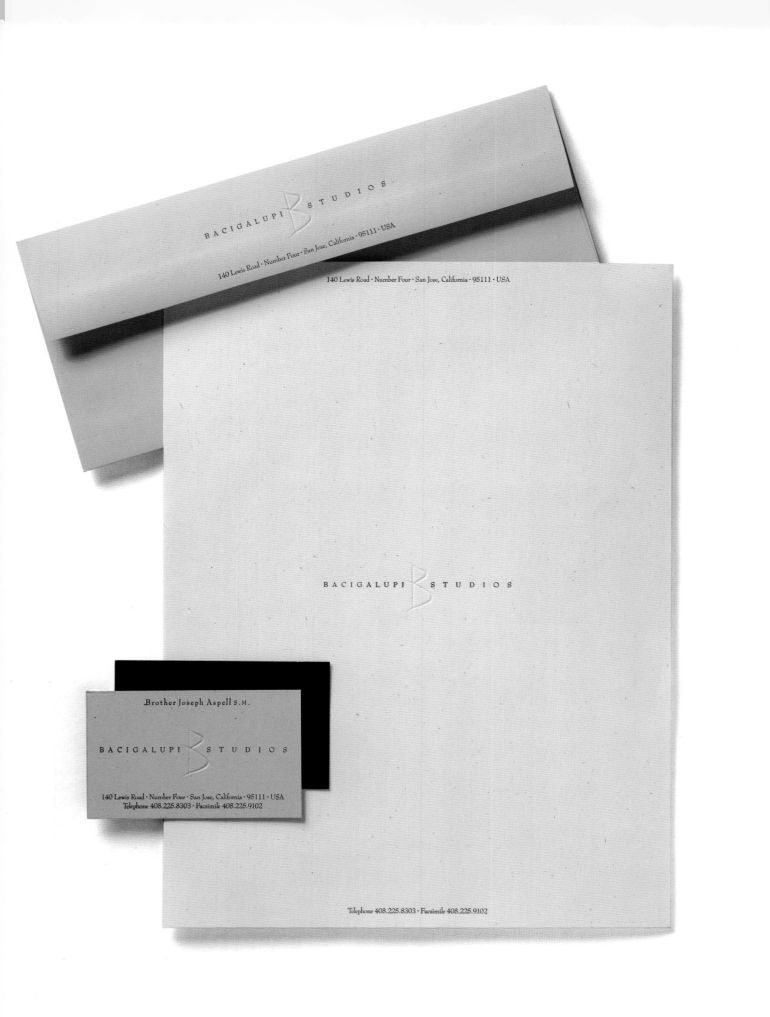

Client: Bacigalupi Studios
Design Firm: Tharp Did It • Los Gatos/San Francisco
Art Director: Rick Tharp
Designers: Rick Tharp, Jana Heer
Paper/Printing: One color and deboss on French Speckletone

Client: Michael Collins & Co.
Design Firm: Emery/Poe Design
Art Director: David Poe
Designer: David Poe
Paper/Printing: Four colors on Neenah Environment

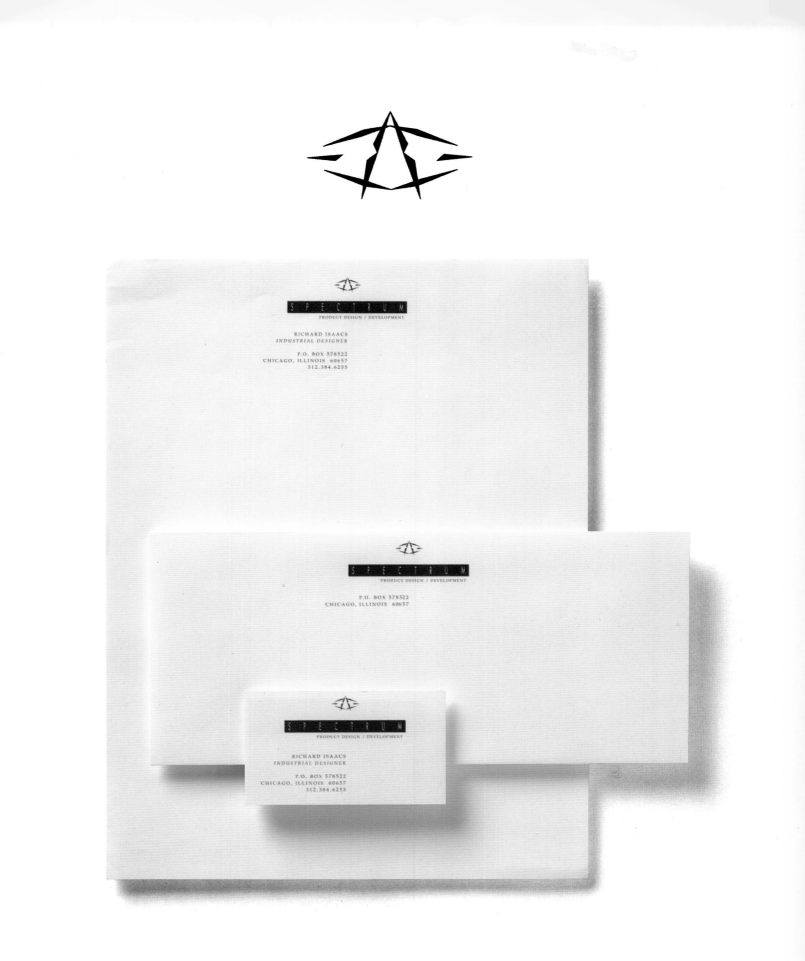

Client: Spectrum Design
Design Firm: CMC Design
Art Director: Chris Cacci
Paper/Printing: One color on Starwhite Vicksburg Natural

Client: Print Northwest
Design Firm: Hornall Anderson Design Works
Art Director: Jack Anderson
Designers: Jack Anderson, Heidi Hatlestad, Jani Drewfs
Airbrush Illustrator: Scott McDougall
Paper/Printing: Six colors on Bank Bond

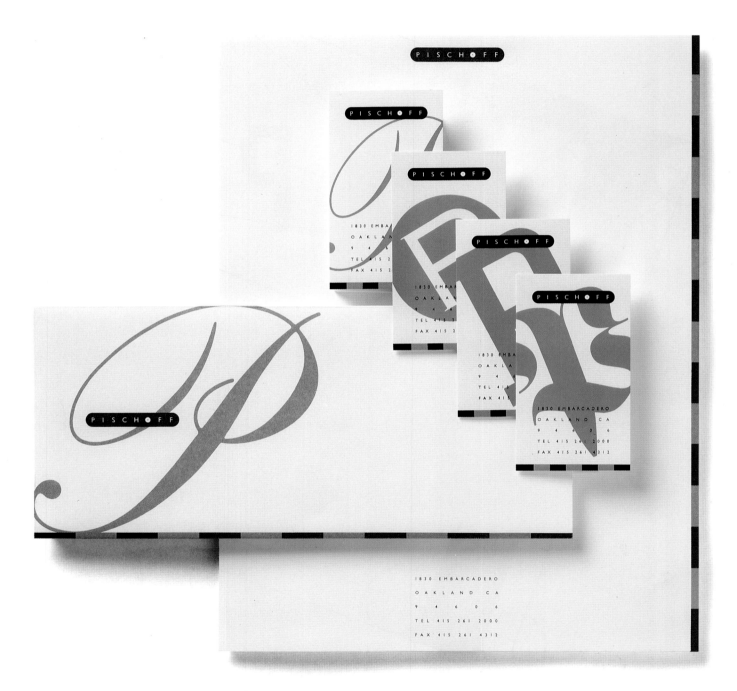

Client: Pischoff Company
Design Firm: Vanderbyl Design
Designer: Michael Vanderbyl
Paper/Printing: Starwhite Vicksburg

Client: MH Concepts International Ltd.
Design Firm: Unlimited Swan, Inc.
Art Director: Jim Swan
Designer: Jim Swan
Illustrator: Jim Swan
Paper/Printing: One color and pearl foil stamp on Classic Linen

Client: Chintz Decor Inc.
Design Firm: Unlimited Swan, Inc.
Art Director: Jim Swan
Designer: Jim Swan
Illustrator: Jim Swan
Paper/Printing: Three colors on Classic Linen

CONCEPTS
INTERNATIONAL

MH CONCEPTS INTERNATIONAL, LTD.
209 HARRISON AVENUE, HARRISON, NEW YORK 10528   FAX: 914-835-1023   PHONE: 914-835-5770

Chintz Decor Incorporated
66 Crescent Street
Stamford, CT 06906
203-327-6992

CHINTZ
DECOR

LAURA
SMITH

I
L
L
U
S
T
R
A
T
I
O
N

Mathews
PRINTING

2202 Liberty Avenue
Pittsburgh, PA 15222
(412) 391-9135

F A X
212 627 2916
T E L
12 EAST 14TH STREET NEW YORK, N.Y. 10003   212 206 9162

Client: Laura Smith Illustration
Design Firm: Michael Doret, Inc.
Art Director: Michael Doret
Designer: Michael Doret
Lettering: Michael Doret
Paper/Printing: Two colors on Gilcrest Laid

Client: Mathews Printing
Design Firm: Adam, Filippo & Associates
Art Director: Robert Adam
Designer: Barbara S. Peak
Paper/Printing: Two colors on Simpson Filare Script Natural White

Client: Trade-Marx
Design Firm: Rick Eiber Design (RED)
Art Director: Rick Eiber
Designer: Rick Eiber
Illustrator: Norman Hathaway
Paper/Printing: Two colors and emboss on Speckletone

GUNNER
PIOTTER
LANDSCAPES
1127 West Chestnut Street Chicago, Illinois 60622

312. 666. 2896

GUNNER
PIOTTER
LANDSCAPES
1127 West Chestnut Street Chicago, Illinois 60622

GUNNER
PIOTTER
LANDSCAPES
1127 West Chestnut Street Chicago, Illinois 60622

312. 666. 2896

Client: Gunner Piotter Landscapes
Design Firm: Condon Norman Design
Art Director: Phylane Norman
Designer: Michael Golec
Paper/Printing: One color on French Speckletone

DISTINCTIVE LANDSCAPES

DIVISION of CAROL BARNHART, INC.

Client: Deadline Printing
Design Firm: Identity Center
Art Director: Wayne Kosterman
Designer: John Anderson

Client: Concept Unlimited, Inc.
Design Firm: Turpin Design Associates
Art Director: Tony F. Turpin
Designers: Greg Guhl, Riley Lawhorn, Tony F. Turpin

Client: Distinctive Landscapes
Design Firm: Tollner Design Group
Art Director: Lisa Tollner
Designer: Kim Tucker
Illustrator: Kim Tucker

Client: Anderson Interiors
Design Firm: Adam, Filippo & Associates
Art Director: Ralph James Russini
Designers: Barabara S. Peak, Alyce Nadine Hoggan, Sharon L. Bretz

Client: Carol Barnhart, Inc.
Design Firm: Greene Art Associates
Art Director: Hester Greene
Designer: Hester Greene

Client: Sacramento Valley Production Theatre Company
Design Firm: Page Design, Inc.
Art Director: Paul Page
Designer: Paula Sugarman
Illustrator: Paula Sugarman

10. MANUFACTURING / INDUSTRY

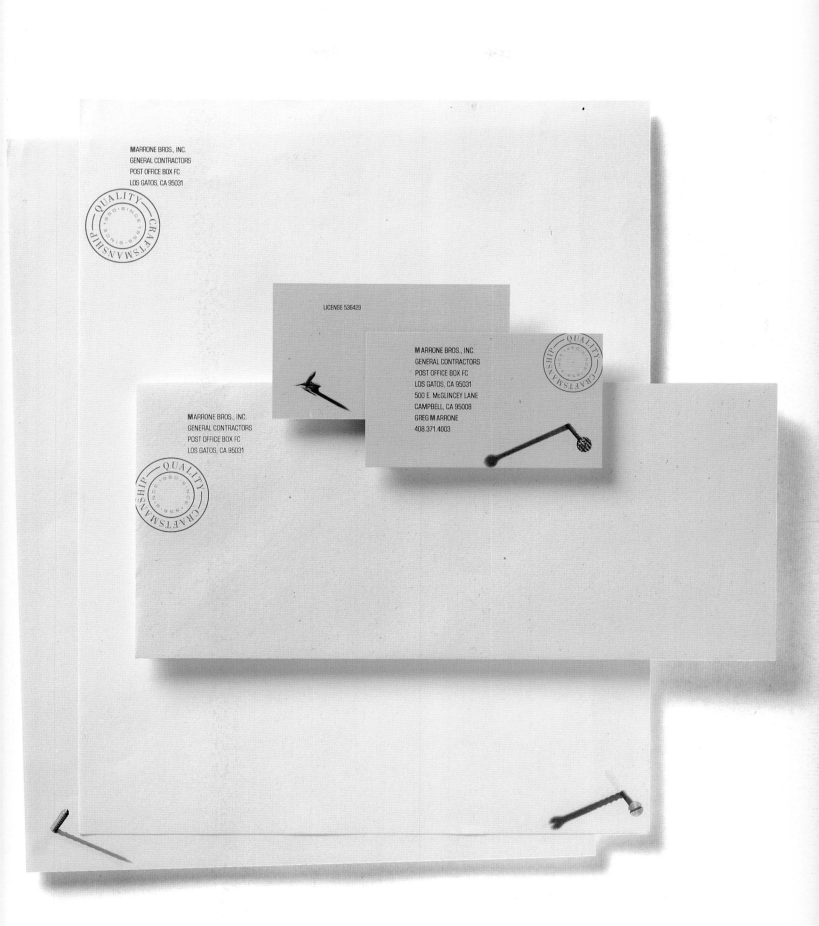

Client: Marrone Brothers Construction
Design Firm: Tharp Did It • Los Gatos/San Francisco
Art Director: Rick Tharp
Designer: Rick Tharp
Paper/Printing: Two colors on Simpson Protocol

167 Milk Street, Suite 185
Boston, Massachusetts
02109-4315

617 243 4383 Tel
617 737 8118 Fax

GREAT BRITISH KETTLES LTD

167 Milk Street, Suite 185
Boston, Massachusetts
02109-4315

GREAT BRITISH KETTLES LTD

J. GERARD CREGAN
Vice President

167 Milk Street, Suite 185
Boston, Massachusetts
02109-4315
617 243 4383 Tel
617 737 8118 Fax

GREAT BRITISH KETTLES LTD

167 Milk Street, Suite 185
Boston, Massachusetts
02109-4315

GREAT BRITISH KETTLES LTD

Client: Great British Kettles Ltd.
Design Firm: Fitch Richardson Smith
Art Director: Ann Gildea
Designer: Katie Murphy
Paper/Printing: Two colors on Champion Benefit Recycled

radius

Radius, Inc.
404 E. Plumeria Drive
San Jose, CA
95134
(408) 434-1010
FAX: (408) 434-0770

Linda Wilkin
Engineering Services Manager
Radius, Inc.
404 E. Plumeria Drive
San Jose, CA
95134
(408) 434-1010
FAX: (408) 434-0770

radius

radius

Radius, Inc.
404 E. Plumeria Drive
San Jose, CA
95134

Client: Radius, Inc.
Design Firm: Mortensen Design
Art Director: Gordon Mortensen
Designer: Gordon Mortensen
Paper/Printing: Three colors on Protocol 100 Ivory

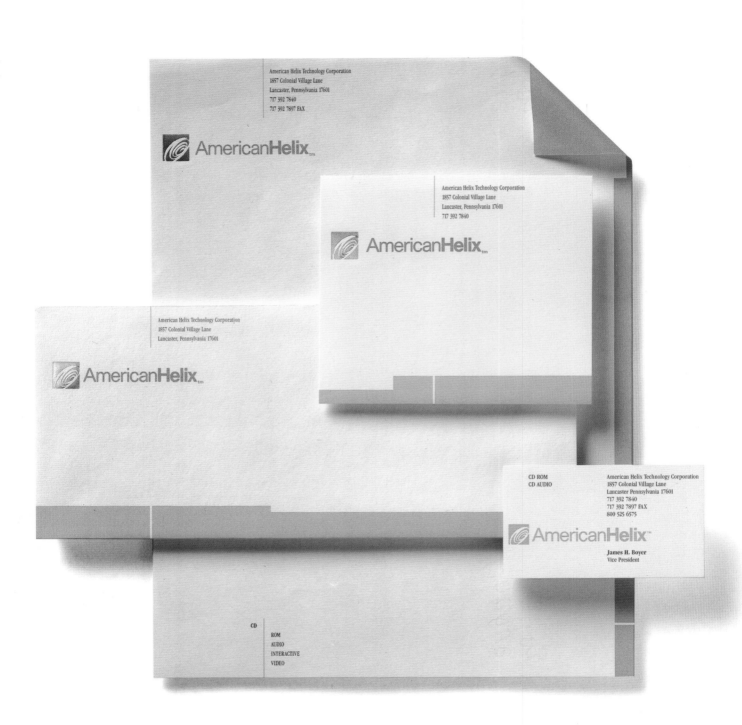

Client: American Helix Technology
Design Firm: Musser Design
Art Director: Musser
Designer: Musser
Paper/Printing: Three colors and foil on Neenah Opaque

Client: Bayoil (USA) Inc.
Design Firm: Unlimited Swan, Inc.
Art Director: Jim Swan
Designer: Jim Swan
Illustrator: Jim Swan
Paper/Printing: Two colors on Mohawk Superfine

Client: REBARN
Design Firm: F. Eugene Smith Design Management
Art Director: F. Eugene Smith
Designer: Carlo Piech
Paper/Printing: Two colors on French Speckletone Natural Text

Client: Ray's Welding Inc.
Design Firm: Lancaster Design & Art, Inc.
Art Director: Kevin Ranck
Designer: Carolyn Mosher
Paper/Printing: Two colors on Kilmory Script

Client: Procoil
Design Firm: Adam Filippo & Associates
Art Director: Robert Adam
Designer: Adam Filippo & Associates
Paper/Printing: Two colors on Strathmore Writing Bright White Laid

Client: Tektronix, Inc.
Design Firm: Robert Bailey Inc.
Art Director: Robert Bailey
Designer: Robert Bailey, Carolyn Coghlan
Paper/Printing: Five colors on Lustro Gloss

SUGARTREE

SUGARTREE

SUGARTREE

DAVID H. COLTON
President
SugarTree International

1035 PEARL STREET
BOULDER COLORADO USA 80302
303 447 3068   FAX 303 449 3095

1035 PEARL STREET 5TH FLOOR   BOULDER COLORADO USA 80302   303 447 3068   FAX 303 449 2773

Client: Astarte, Inc.
Design Firm: Communication Arts Inc.
Art Director: Richard Foy
Designer: Hugh Enockson
Paper/Printing: Two color on Starwhite Vicksburg Archiva

Client: Cubi Clip
Design Firm: Tollner Design Group
Art Director: Lisa Tollner
Designer: Kim Tucker
Illustrator: Kim Tucker

Client: Laminated Papers Inc.
Design Firm: Cipriani Kremer Design
Art Director: Robert Cipriani
Paper/Printing: Three colors on Crane's Crest

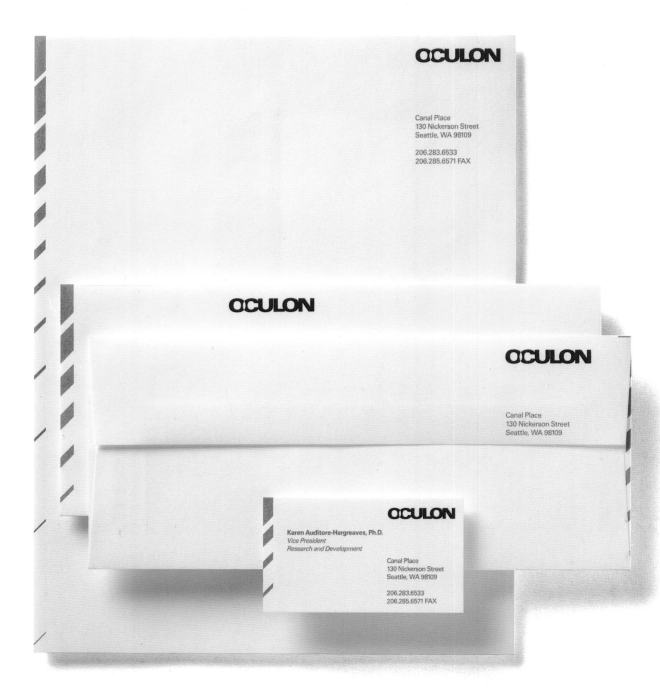

Client: Oculon, Inc.
Design Firm: Rick Eiber Design (RED)
Art Director: Rick Eiber
Designer: Eric Janssen
Paper/Printing: Two colors on Classic Crest

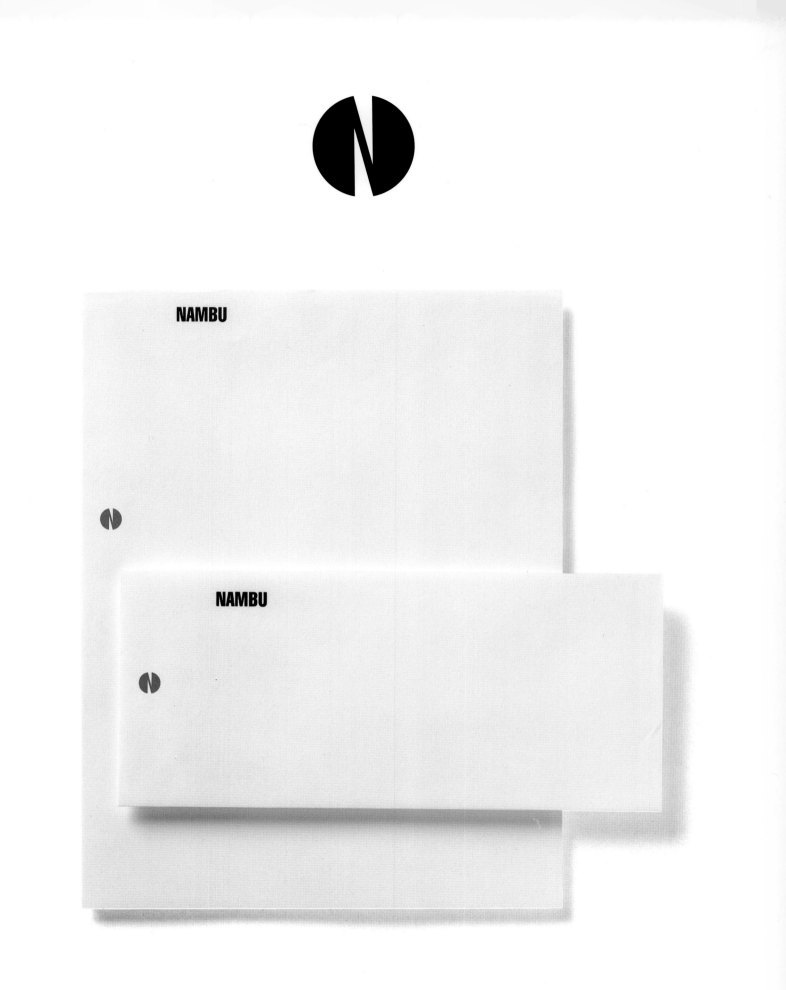

Client: Nambu International, Inc.
Design Firm: Donovan and Green
Art Director: Nancye Green
Designers: Clint Morgan, Dennis Favello
Paper/Printing: Two colors on Crane's Crest Fluorescent White Opaque Wove

KINEO
DESIGN BY F·A·PORSCHE

KINEO
DESIGN BY F·A·PORSCHE

KINEO
DESIGN BY F·A·PORSCHE

Gerald Berton
President

*Kineo USA Ltd
141 East Boston Post Road
Mamaroneck, New York
10543*

*Telephone 914 381 5100
Fax 914 698 3893*

*Kineo USA Ltd
141 East Boston Post Road
Mamaroneck, New York
10543*

*Telephone 914 381 5100
Fax 914 698 3893*

Client: Kineo
Design Firm: Donovan and Green
Art Directors: Michael Green, Nancye Green
Designer: Clint Morgan
Paper/Printing: Three colors on Strathmore Writing

26 Landsdowne Street
Cambridge
Massachusetts
02139 4234
U.S.A.

Telephone
617 494 0171
Facsimile
617 494 9263

Alkermes

26 Landsdowne Street
Cambridge
Massachusetts
02139 4234
U.S.A.

Alkermes

26 Landsdowne Street
Cambridge
Massachusetts
02139 4234
U.S.A.

Alkermes

Laura A. McCarroll, M.S.
Senior Research Associate
and Laboratory Manager

Alkermes

26 Landsdowne Street
Cambridge
Massachusetts
02139 4234
U.S.A.

Telephone
617 494 0171
Facsimile
617 494 9263

Client: Alkermes, Inc.
Design Firm: Katz Wheeler Design
Art Director: Joel Katz
Designer: Annette Chang Vander
Paper/Printing: One color and embossing on Strathmore Writing

Client: A.G. Heinze Inc.
Design Firm: Mark Palmer Design
Art Director: Mark Palmer
Designer: Mark Palmer
Computer Production: Curtis Palmer
Paper/Printing: Two colors on Strathmore Writing Wove

Client: National Steel Corporation
Design Firm: Adam, Filippo & Associates
Art Director: Robert Adam
Designers: Robert Adam, Ralph James Russini
Paper/Printing: Two colors on Simpson Filare Script Bianco White

Client: Consumer Connection
Design Firm: Mark Palmer Design
Art Director: Mark Palmer
Designer: Mark Palmer
Computer Production: Curtis Palmer
Paper/Printing: Simpson Gainsborough

Client: Rodgers Instrument Corp.
Design Firm: Robert Bailey Inc.
Art Director: Robert Bailey
Designer: Carolyn Coghlan
Paper/Printing: Simpson Protocol Writing

ADVANCE
FIRE EXTINGUISHER COMPANY

P.O. BOX 478

ISSAQUAH, WA 98027-0478

747.3008 • 1.800.427.6818

ADVANCE
FIRE EXTINGUISHER COMPANY

P.O. BOX 478

ISSAQUAH, WA

98027-0478

ADVANCE
FIRE EXTINGUISHER COMPANY

BOB VESELY, OPERATIONS MANAGER
P.O. BOX 478 • ISSAQUAH, WA 98027 • 747.3008 • 1.800.427.6818

Client: Advance Fire Extinguisher Co.
Design Firm: G.T. Rapp & Company
Art Director: Liz Kearney
Designer: Margo Christianson
Paper/Printing: Two colors on Gilbert Neu-Tech Ultra White Wove

Joint Venture Corporation of Westinghouse, General Electric, and Mitsubishi.

Powerex, Inc.
Hillis Street
Youngwood, Pennsylvania 15697
(412) 925-7272

Ronald C. Whigham
President &
Chief Executive Officer

Powerex, Inc.
Hillis Street
Youngwood, PA 15697

Joint Venture Corporation of Westinghouse, General Electric and Mitsubishi.

Ronald C. Whigham

President &
Chief Executive Officer

Joint Venture Corporation of Westinghouse, General Electric, and Mitsubishi.

Powerex, Inc.
Hillis Street
Youngwood, PA 15697
(412) 925-4400

James R. Myler

Vice President &
Chief Financial Officer

Joint Venture Corporation of Westinghouse, General Electric, and Mitsubishi.

Powerex, Inc.
Hillis Street
Youngwood, PA 15697
(412) 925-4332

Ronald C. Whigham

President &
Chief Executive Officer

Joint Venture Corporation of Westinghouse, General Electric, and Mitsubishi.

Powerex, Inc.
Youngwood
Pennsylvania 15697
(412) 925-4400

Client: Powerex, Inc.
Design Firm: Adam, Filippo & Associates
Art Director: Adam, Filippo & Associates
Designer: Adam, Filippo & Associates
Paper/Printing: Two colors on Simpson Filare Script Bianco White

Client: Esmark Apparel, Inc.
Design Firm: Barry David Berger + Assoc., Inc.
Art Director: Barry Berger
Designers: Sharon Reiter, Cheryl Oppenheim
Paper/Printing: One color

Client: Leonard's Metal, Inc.
Design Firm: Intelplex
Art Director: Alan Sherman
Designer: Neil Koenig
Production: Studio One

GEORGETOWN UNIMETAL

GEORGETOWN UNIMETAL

Georgetown Unimetal Sales
1901 Roxborough Rd. Suite 220
Charlotte, NC 28211

Charles A. Cameron
Regional Sales Manager

GEORGETOWN UNIMETAL

(803) 546-0239

Georgetown Unimetal Sales
Marketing Unimetal and Georgetown Steel
Corporation Wire Rods in the U.S.A.

GEORGETOWN UNIMETAL

Marketing Unimetal and
Georgetown Steel Corporation
Wire Rods in the U.S.A.

Georgetown Unimetal Sales
1901 Roxborough Rd. Suite 220
Charlotte, NC 28211

Phone: (704) 365-2205
        (800) 327-0558
Fax: (704) 365-1733

Client: Georgetown Unimetal Sales
Design Firm: Design/Joe Sonderman, Inc.
Designer: Tim Gilland
Paper/Printing: Three colors

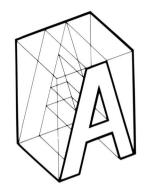

Client: Rafn
Design Firm: Hornall Anderson Design Works
Art Director: Jack Anderson
Designers: Jack Anderson, Jani Drewfs, David Bates, Brian O'Neill
Illustrator: Brian O'Neill

Client: Astor Construction
Design Firm: Greene Art Associates
Art Director: Hester Greene
Designer: Peter Greene

Client: Climatech, Inc.
Design Firm: Adam, Filippo & Associates
Art Director: Adam, Filippo & Associates
Designer: Ralph James Russini

Client: Minko Construction Co.
Design Firm: Design Center
Art Director: John Reger
Designer: Todd Spichke

Client: Transtar, Inc.
Design Firm: Adam, Filippo & Associates
Art Director: Robert Adam
Designer: Barbara S. Peak

Client: E.I. duPont de Nemours & Co., Inc.
Design Firm: Richard Danne & Associates Inc
Art Director: Richard Danne
Designer: Gary Skeggs

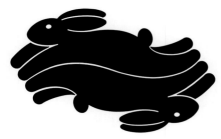

Client: Valley Papers
Design Firm: J. Brelsford Design, Inc.
Art Director: Jerry Brelsford
Designer: Jerry Brelsford

Client: Valsan
Design Firm: Rowe & Ballantine
Art Director: Edward L. Rowe, Jr.
Designer: John H. Ballantine

Client: 3M Company
Design Firm: Design Center
Art Director: John Reger

Client: SmithKline Corporation
Design Firm: Frank D'Astolfo Design
Art Director: Frank D'Astolfo
Designer: Frank D'Astolfo

Client: Rebo Research, Inc.
Design Firm: M Plus M Incorporated
Art Directors: Michael McGinn, Takaaki Matsumoto
Designer: Michael McGinn
Illustrator: Jack Tom

Client: KRW Energy Systems, Inc.
Design Firm: Adam, Filippo & Associates
Art Director: Adam, Filippo & Associates
Designer: Adam, Filippo & Associates

11. HEALTH CARE

Deutsches Altenheim

2222 Centre Street
West Roxbury, MA 02132
(617) 325-1230

Deutsches Altenheim

Capital Campaign Office
165 Newbury Street
Boston, MA 02116
(617) 266-6411

Deutsches Altenheim

2222 Centre Street
West Roxbury, MA 02132
(617) 325-1230

Heinrich Brinkhaus
President

Deutsches Altenheim

2222 Centre Street
West Roxbury, MA 02132
(617) 325-1230

Client: Deutsches Altenheim (German Home for the Aged)
Design Firm: Fitch Richardson Smith Inc.
Art Director: Patty O'Leary
Designer: Patty O'Leary
Illustrator: Patty O'Leary
Paper/Printing: Two colors on Champion Benefit

OPHTHALMIC INFORMATION SYSTEMS

34 Market Place, Suite 330
Baltimore, Maryland 21202
301-625-0565

OPHTHALMIC INFORMATION SYSTEMS

34 Market Place, Suite 330
Baltimore, Maryland 21202

Bert M. Glaser, M.D.

OPHTHALMIC INFORMATION SYSTEMS

34 Market Place, Suite 330
Baltimore, Maryland 21202
301-625-0565

Client: Opthalmic Information Systems
Design Firm: Joseph Dieter Visual Communications
Art Director: Joseph M. Dieter, Jr.
Designer: Joseph M. Dieter, Jr.
Paper/Printing: Two colors on Strathmore Writing

Surgical Design Corporation
4253 21st Street
L.I.C., New York 11101
(718) 392-5022
(800) 458-4344
Telex 141095 Surg Design

Setting the Standard
in Intraocular Microsurgery
Since 1968

✪ **Surgical Design**

✪ **Surgical Design**

Surgical Design Corporation
4253 21st Street
L.I.C., New York 11101

✪ **Surgical Design**

Setting the Standard
in Intraocular Microsurgery
Since 1968

Surgical Design Corporation
4253 21st Street
L.I.C., New York 11101
(718) 392-5022
(800) 458-4344
Telex 141095 Surg Design

Andrew P. Greenberg
Chief Financial Officer

Client: Surgical Design Corporation
Design Firm: Richard Danne & Associates, Inc.
Art Director: Richard Danne
Designer: Richard Danne
Paper/Printing: One color on Strathmore Writing

Client: Belton Dickinson
Design Firm: Ellis • Pratt Design
Art Director: Vernon Ellis
Designer: Tim Coletti
Paper/Printing: Three colors on Curtis Linen

Ross F. Marchetta M.D.

Obstetrics and Gynecology of Bath, Inc
799 Wye Road
Akron, Ohio
44333-2268

Ross F. Marchetta M.D.

Obstetrics and Gynecology of Bath, Inc
799 Wye Road
Akron, Ohio 44333
216/666/1166
800/443/7222
216/668/3919 FAX

Ross F. Marchetta M.D.

Obstetrics and Gynecology of Bath, Inc
799 Wye Road
Akron, Ohio 44333
216/666/1166
800/443/7222
216/668/3919 FAX

Client: Dr. Ross Marchetta
Design Firm: F. Eugene Smith Design Management, Inc.
Art Director: F. Eugune Smith
Designer: Carlo Piech
Paper/Printing: Two colors on Classic Crest Writing Classic Natural White

Client: Wyman Park Medical Center
Design Firm: Art As Applied To Medicine, Johns Hopkins Medical Institutions
Art Director: Joseph M. Dieter, Jr.
Designer: Joseph M. Dieter, Jr.
Paper/Printing: Two colors on Strathmore Writing

Client: Heartland Institute For Health
Design Firm: Turpin Design Associates
Art Director: Tony F. Turpin
Designer: Tony F. Turpin
Paper/Printing: Two colors on Strathmore Writing

Elders at WORK

in Baltimore!

a service of The Johns Hopkins Medical Institutions

Wyman Park Medical Center · 3100 Wyman Park Drive · Baltimore, Maryland 21211
301-338-3663 · 301-955-0975

HEARTLAND
INSTITUTE FOR HEALTH

Rt. 3, Mars Hill, North Carolina 28754
(704) 689-4998

A division of K&K Health Centers, Inc.

L.S.A.
Family
Health
Service

Sr. Janet McCann, L.S.A.
President
Anna Lou Delavenson, Ph.D.
Secretary
Sr. M. Robert Nagle, RN, M.Ed.
Treasurer

BOARD OF DIRECTORS
Richard J. Bonforte, M.D.
Chairperson
Yvonne Aliotano
Patricia R. Barry
Byron Irwin Chandler
Howard G. Estock, Esq.
Elizabeth F. Farling
Alice R. Pettey
Rosemarie C. McGrath
June Z. Moss, Ph.D.
Elizabeth Murphy, RN
Rev. Leroy Rickey
Andrew A. Ross
Ralph A. Siciliano, Esq.
George N. Sisnsbely

FOUNDING MEMBER
William J. Doyle

CO-DIRECTORS
Marion Ebner
Sr. Judith Garson

Little Sisters
of the Assumption
Family Health
Service

426 East 119 Street
New York, NY 10035
212-289-6484

SAVING SIGHT

Maryland Society for the Prevention of Blindness

1313 West Old Cold Spring Lane   Baltimore, Maryland 21209   (301) 243-2201

Client: LSA Family Health Service
Design Firm: Stillman Design Associates
Art Director: Linda Stillman
Designer: Carol Baxter
Illustrator: Connie Circosta
Paper/Printing: Two colors on Gilbert Writing Wove

Client: Maryland Society For The Prevention of Blindness
Design Firm: Joseph Dieter Visual Communications
Art Director: Joseph M. Dieter, Jr.
Designer: Joseph M. Dieter, Jr.
Paper/Printing: Four colors on Strathmore Writing

MEDICAL SPECIALTY
GROUP

Medical Specialty Group, Inc.
Kerrigan's Corner
2 Reedsdale Road
Milton, MA 02186
(617) 698-0715
FAX: (617) 698-7559

1093 North Main Street
Randolph, MA 02368
(617) 961-1450

577 East Broadway
South Boston, MA 02127
(617) 698-0715

Richard M. Delany, M.D., F.A.C.C.
Cardiology
Internal Medicine

Scott B. Lutch, M.D.
Cardiology
Internal Medicine

George L. Barrett, M.D.
Gastroenterology
Internal Medicine

MEDICAL SPECIALTY
GROUP

Kerrigan's Corner
2 Reedsdale Road
Milton, MA 02186
(617) 698-0715
FAX: (617) 698-7559

1093 North Main Street
Randolph, MA 02368
(617) 961-1450

George L. Barrett, M.D.
Gastroenterology
Internal Medicine

577 East Broadway
South Boston, MA 02127
(617) 698-0715

MEDICAL SPECIALTY
GROUP

Kerrigan's Corner
2 Reedsdale Road
Milton, MA 02186

Client:	Medical Specialty Group Inc.
Agency:	Kennedy & Company
Design Firm:	Letvin Design
Art Director:	Carolyn Letvin
Designer:	Carolyn Letvin
Paper/Printing:	Two colors on Strathmore Writing

PENICK
MEMORIAL HOME

*The Episcopal Home for
the Ageing in the Diocese
of North Carolina, Inc.*

PENICK
MEMORIAL HOME

Saint Peter's Nursing Center
Kinder Elder Kare

East Rhode Island Avenue Extension
Post Office Box 2001
Southern Pines, NC 28388

Saint Peter's Nursing Center

Kinder Elder Kare

East Rhode Island Avenue Extension
Post Office Box 2001
Southern Pines, NC 28388
919•692•0300
Fax 919•692•8287

Client: Ruder•Finn
Design Firm: Sally Johns Design Studio
Art Director: Sally Johns
Designer: Jeff Dale
Illustrator: Jeff Dale
Paper/Printing: Two colors on Neenah Classic Laid

AKRON
F A M I L Y
D E N T I S T
JOHN T. GOTWALT, D.D.S.

AKRON
F A M I L Y
D E N T I S T
JOHN T. GOTWALT, D.D.S.

112 South 7th Street
Akron, PA 17501
717-859-2013

AKRON
F A M I L Y
D E N T I S T
JOHN T. GOTWALT, D.D.S.

112 South 7th Street
Akron, PA 17501
717-859-2013

112 South 7th Street
Akron, PA 17501
717-859-2013

Client:	Akron Family Dentist
Design Firm:	Lancaster Design & Art, Inc.
Art Director:	Drew Tyson
Designer:	Kevin Ranck
Illustrator:	Carolyn Mosher
Paper/Printing:	Two colors on Neenah Classic Laid

Lancaster
PERIODONTAL
Associates

ARTHUR H. SOMMER, D.M.D.

Lancaster
PERIODONTAL
Associates

ARTHUR H. SOMMER, D.M.D.

131 FOXSHIRE DRIVE
LANCASTER, PA 17601

717-560-9191

131 FOXSHIRE DRIVE, LANCASTER, PA 17601   717-560-9191

Client: Lancaster Periodontal Associates
Design Firm: Lancaster Design & Art
Art Director: Drew Tyson
Designer: Amelia Rockwell-Seton
Paper/Printing: Two colors on Gilbert Writing

MASSAGE THERAPY CENTER OF WINNETKA

MASSAGE THERAPY CENTER OF WINNETKA

MASSAGE
THERAPY
CENTER
OF
WINNETKA

JOHN G. LOUIS, C.M.T.
DIRECTOR

40 GREEN BAY ROAD
WINNETKA, ILLINOIS 60093
708.446.5700

40 GREEN BAY ROAD
WINNETKA, ILLINOIS 60093
708.446.5700

Client: Massage Therapy Center of Winnetka
Design Firm: Michael Stanard Inc.
Art Director: Michael Stanard
Designer: Marcos Chavez
Paper/Printing: Two colors on Strathmore Writing

Client: Summa Health System
Design Firm: Adam, Filippo & Associates
Art Director: Robert Adam
Designer: Barbara S. Peak, Ralph James Russini
Paper/Printing: Three colors on Neenah Classic Laid

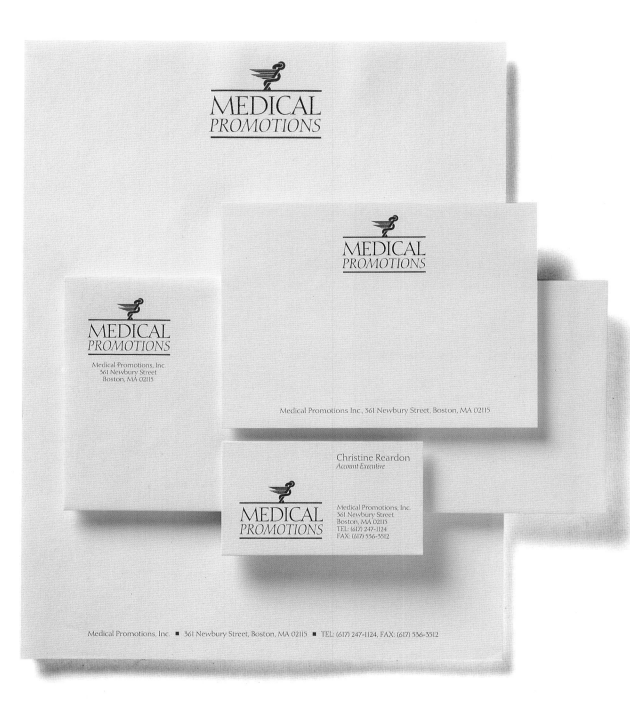

Medical Promotions, Inc. ■ 361 Newbury Street, Boston, MA 02115 ■ TEL: (617) 247-1124, FAX: (617) 536-3512

Client:	Medical Promotions, Inc.
Agency:	Kennedy & Company
Design Firm:	Letvin Design
Art Director:	Carolyn Letvin
Designer:	Carolyn Letvin
Paper/Printing:	Two colors on Strathmore Writing

Client: Hillhaven Corporation
Design Firm: Hornall Anderson Design Works
Art Director: Jack Anderson
Designers: Jack Anderson, Mary Hermes,
David Bates

Client: Victim Services
Design Firm: J. Brelsford Design, Inc.
Art Director: Jerry Brelsford
Designer: Jerry Brelsford

Client: Boston Eye Surgery & Laser Center
Agency: Kennedy & Company
Design Firm: Letvin Design
Art Director: Carolyn Letvin
Designer: Carolyn Letvin

Client: Catholic Healthcare West
Design Firm: Page Design, Inc.
Art Director: Paul Page
Designer: Paula Sugarman

Client: Mercy San Juan Hospital
Design Firm: Page Design, Inc.
Art Director: Paul Page
Designer: Paula Sugarman
Illustrator: Paula Sugarman

Client: American Association of Spinal
Cord Injury Nurses
Design Firm: Frank D'Astolfo Design
Art Director: Frank D'Astolfo
Designer: Frank D'Astolfo

12. EDUCATION / NON-PROFIT

Client: Western Regional Greek Conference
Design Firm: Sayles Graphic Design
Art Director: John Sayles
Designer: John Sayles
Paper/Printing: Two colors on French Speckletone

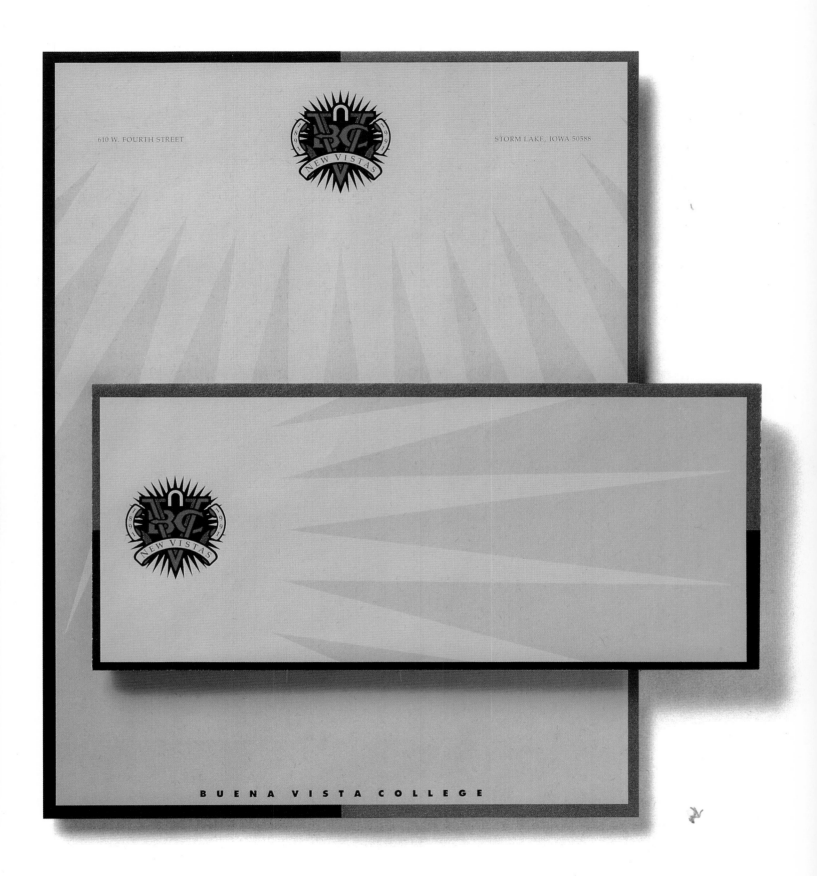

610 W. FOURTH STREET

STORM LAKE, IOWA 50588

NEW VISTAS

NEW VISTAS

BUENA VISTA COLLEGE

Client: Buena Vista College
Design Firm: Sayles Graphic Design
Art Director: John Sayles
Designer: John Sayles
Paper/Printing: Four colors on James River (Special Order)

Client: California School Leadership Academy
Design Firm: Marketing By Design
Art Director: Joel Stinghen
Designer: Joel Stinghen
Illustrator: Joel Stinghen
Paper/Printing: Two colors on Classic Crest

Los Marineros
113 Harbor Way
Santa Barbara
California 93109
(805) 966-7107

Los Marineros
113 Harbor Way
Santa Barbara
California 93109
(805) 966-7107
Sheila Cushman
Program Coordinator
Sponsored by the Channel Islands
National Marine Sanctuary and
the Santa Barbara Museum
of Natural History

Sponsored by the Channel Islands National Marine Sanctuary and the Santa Barbara Museum of Natural History

Client: Los Marineros
Design Firm: Puccinelli Design
Art Director: Keith Puccinelli
Designer: Keith Puccinelli
Illustrator: Keith Puccinelli
Paper/Printing: Two colors on Cross Pointe Bond

Friendship One

Around the World
for Kids

Made possible by the
generous support of
United Airlines.

Friendship One

Around the World
for Kids

Friendship Foundation
(A Non-Profit Corporation)

c/o The Museum of Flight
9404 E. Marginal Way S.
Seattle, Washington 98108

Clay Lacy
President

Friendship One

Around the World   c/o The Museum of Flight
for Kids   9404 E. Marginal Way S.
                         Seattle, Washington 98108
Friendship Foundation   (206) 764-5708
(A Non-Profit Corp.)   Fax # (206) 764-5707

Friendship Foundation
(A Non-Profit Corporation)

c/o The Museum of Flight
9404 E. Marginal Way S.
Seattle, Washington 98108
(206) 764-5708
Fax # (206) 764-5707

Client: Museum of Flight
Design Firm: Hornall Anderson Design Works
Art Director: Jack Anderson
Designers: Jack Anderson, Julie Tanagi-Lock
Paper/Printing: Four colors on Protocol Writing

FAMILYFEST

Columbia Point Boston, MA 02125

Family Fest, a family-oriented festival, benefits Ronald McDonald Children's Charities®, and is sponsored by John F. Kennedy Library and Museum, McDonald's®, WMJX 106.7 FM, and WCVB-TV.

Client: JFK Library
Design Firm: WCVB TV Design
Art Director: Marc English
Designer: Marc English
Illustrator: Rebecka, Teena, Marc
Paper/Printing: Five colors on Strathmore Writing

Client: Chicago Historical Society
Design Firm: Donovan and Green
Art Director: Michael Donovan
Designer: Rose Biondi
Paper/Printing: Two colors on Strathmore Wove Bright White

Client: Prairie Fire Rural Action
Design Firm: Identity Center
Art Director: Wayne Kosterman
Designer: Wayne Kosterman
Paper/Printing: Two colors on Strathmore Writing

Client: Alan Keinberg
Design Firm: Anthony McCall Associates
Art Director: Anthony McCall
Designer: Wing Chan
Illustrator: Wing Chan
Paper/Printing: One color on Strathmore Natural White

Client: Queens College
Design Firm: Milton Glaser, Inc.
Art Director: Milton Glaser
Designer: Milton Glaser

Client: The City, Inc.
Design Firm: William Homan Design
Art Director: William Homan
Designer: William Homan

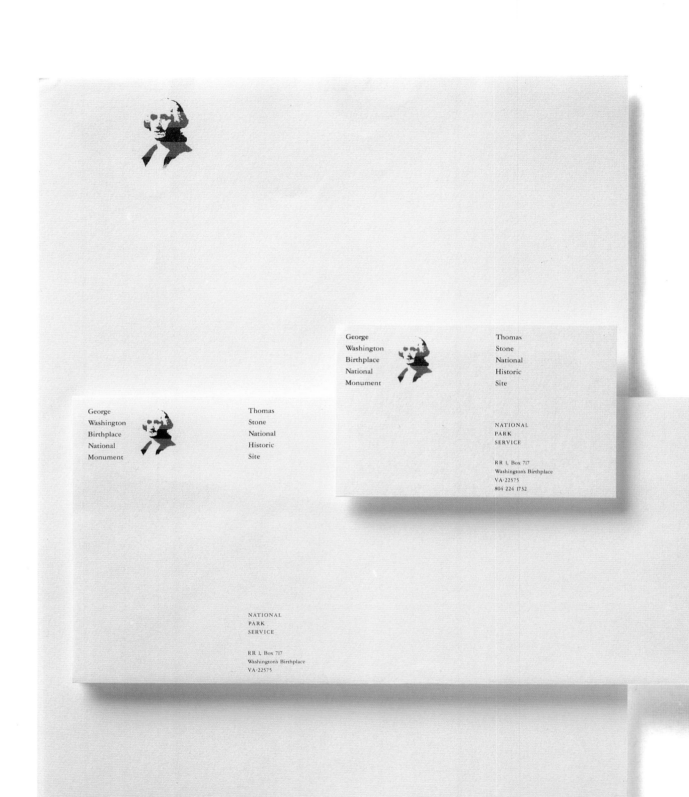

Client: George Washington Birthplace National Monument
Design Firm: Karen Schrader Design
Designer: Karen L. Schrader
Paper/Printing: Three colors on Strathmore Writing

Client: Families and Work Institute
Design Firm: Page, Arbitrio & Resen
Art Director: Kenneth Resen
Designer: Kenneth Resen
Paper/Printing: Three colors

Client: River Heritage
Design Firm: William Homan Design
Art Director: William Homan
Designer: William Homan
Paper/Printing: Three colors

Client: Ruder•Finn
Design Firm: Sally Johns Design Studio
Art Director: Sally Johns
Designer: Jeff Dale
Illustrator: Jeff Dale
Paper/Printing: Two colors on Neenah Environment Recycled

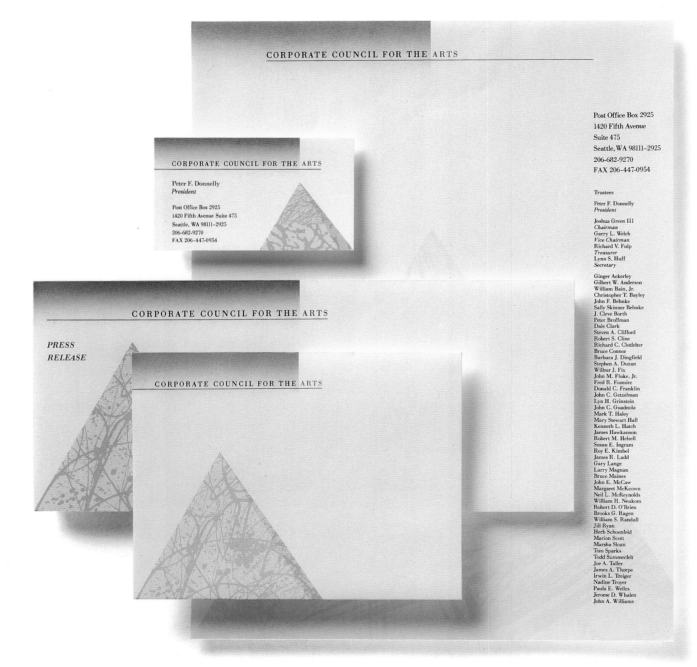

Client: Corporate Council For The Arts
Design Firm: Rick Eiber Design (RED)
Art Director: Rick Eiber
Designer: Ken Shafer
Paper/Printing: Two colors on Classic Crest

Children's AIDS Network
21 Washington Place, New York, NY 10003

Children's AIDS Network
21 Washington Place, New York, NY 10003, (212) 415-6515

Bryan Miskie, Founder, Chairman

Board of Directors: Elaine Herman   Bob Roberts   Mike Denhoff   Jonathan Annis, M.D.   Deanna Annis   Maurice Cohen   Ronald H. Miskie   Armand DiCarlo

Advisory Board: James M. Oleske, M.D., M.P.H.   Margaret C. Heagarty, M.D.   Louis Dell'Olio   Irwin Kellner, Ph.D.   Stephen Nicholas, M.D.   John J. Hutchings, M.D.

Client:	Childrens Aids Network
Design Firm:	The Pushpin Group
Art Director:	Seymour Chwast
Designer:	Seymour Chwast
Illustrator:	Seymour Chwast

Executive Leadership Center

CHELSEA DAY SCHOOL

PULSE OF LOUISIANA

The FRIENDS of the BEVERLY HILLS PUBLIC LIBRARY

deci.mal

Client: California School Leadership Academy
Design Firm: Marketing By Design
Art Director: Joel Stinghen
Designer: Joel Stinghen
Illustrator: Joel Stinghen

Client: Chelsea Day School
Design Firm: Anthony McCall Associates
Art Director: Wing Chan
Designer: Wing Chan
Illustrator: Wing Chan

Client: Pulse Of Louisiana
Design Firm: Whitmer Design
Art Director: Robert H. Whitmer
Designer: Robert H. Whitmer

Client: Friends of the Beverly Hills Public Library
Design Firm: Westwood & Associates
Art Director: David Westwood
Designer: David Westwood

Client: Morris Scholarship Fund
Design Firm: J. Brelsford Design, Inc.
Art Director: Jerry Brelsford
Designer: Jerry Brelsford

Client: Society of Librarians
Design Firm: Kuo Design Group
Art Director: Samuel Kuo
Designer: Samuel Kuo

OREGON COAST
AQUARIUM

SOW
FOR
A DOUBLE HARVEST

UNCCHARLOTTE

ADOPT-A-HIGHWAY

Client: Oregon Coast Aquarium
Design Firm: Robert Bailey, Inc.
Art Director: Robert Bailey
Designers: Carolyn Coghlan, John Williams

Client: Wheat Ridge Foundation
Design Firm: Identity Center
Art Director: Wayne Kosterman
Designer: Wayne Kosterman
Illusrator: Wayne Kosterman

Client: Bay Area Discovery Museum
Design Firm: The Pushpin Group
Art Director: Seymour Chwast
Designer: Seymour Chwast

Client: University Of North Carolina at Charlotte
Design Firm: Design/Joe Sonderman, Inc.
Art Director: Tim Gilland
Designer: Andy Crews

Client: Georgia Power Company
Design Firm: Rousso+Associates, Inc.
Art Director: Steve Rousso
Designer: Steve Rousso

Client: Caltrans
Design Firm: Page Design, Inc.
Art Director: Paul Page
Designer: Tracy Titus

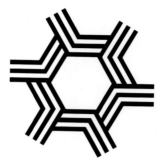

DOME TO DELTA

CUSHING
ACADEMY

EUREEKA'S
CASTLE

Client: SPACES (Saving and Preserving American Cultural Environments)
Design Firm: Porter/Matjasich & Associates
Art Director: Allen Porter
Designer: Allen Porter

Client: Dome To Delta Run
Design Firm: Page Design, Inc.
Art Director: Paul Page
Designer: Brad Maur
Illustrator: Brad Maur

Client: Cushing Academy
Design Firm: Portfolio
Art Director: Bonnie Mineo
Designer: Busha Husak
Illustrator: Busha Husak

Client: Forbes Magazine
Design Firm: De Martino Design Inc.
Art Director: Erick De Martino
Designer: Erick De Martino
Illustrator: Erick De Martino

Client: Nickelodeon
Design Firm: The Pushpin Group
Art Director: Seymour Chwast
Designer: Seymour Chwast
Illustrator: Seymour Chwast

Client: Friends of the Islamorada Area State Parks
Design Firm: M Plus M Incorporated
Art Directors: Michael McGinn, Takaaki Matsumoto
Designer: Michael McGinn

13. MISCELLANEOUS

32 East 57th Street
New York, NY 10022

Telephone: 212 308-6200
Facsimile: 212 308-6218

32 East 57th Street
New York, NY 10022

Telephone: 212 308-6200
Facsimile: 212 308-6218

Martin L. Chaisson
Chairman of the Board and
Co-Chief Executive Officer

32 East 57th Street
New York, NY 10022

Martin L. Chaisson

32 East 57th Street
New York, NY 10022

Client: EventMedia International, Inc.
Design Firm: Michael Doret, Inc.
Art Director: Michael Doret
Designer: Michael Doret
Lettering: Michael Doret
Paper/Printing: Five colors on Crane's Crest

THOMAS J. SHOOK
Director of Promotional Events

2445 Belmont Avenue
P. O. Box 2186 • Youngstown, OH
44504-0186 • (216) 747-2661

2445 Belmont Avenue
P. O. Box 2186
Youngstown, OH 44504-0186

2445 Belmont Avenue
P. O. Box 2186 • Youngstown, OH
44504-0186 • (216) 747-2661

Client: The Cafaro Company
Design Firm: May Design Associates
Art Director: Frederick Mozzy
Designer: Frederick Mozzy
Illustrator: Frederick Mozzy
Paper/Printing: Two colors on Strathmore Writing

Client: San Francisco Opera Guild
Design Firm: Cognata Associates
Art Director: Richard Cognata
Designer: Richard Cognata
Paper/Printing: Two colors

Performing New Music
And Music of The Baroque

Christopher Erede
Music Director

P.O. Box 2256
400 West 43rd Street
Suite 37-N
New York, NY 10036
212 967 7210

Concerto New York Limited

400 West 43rd Street
Suite 37-N
New York, NY 10036

Concerto New York Limited

Client: Concerto NY Ltd.
Design Firm: Lieber Brewster Corporate Design
Art Director: Anna Lieber
Designer: Anna Lieber
Illustrator: Anna Lieber
Paper/Printing: Two colors on Strathmore Writing

Client: Stratton Resort
Design Firm: Design/Joe Sonderman, Inc.
Art Director: Tim Gilland
Designer: Mary Head
Paper/Printing: Three colors on Classic Crest

Client: Pacific Guest Suites
Design Firm: Hornall Anderson Design Works
Art Director: Julia LaPine
Designer: Julia LaPine
Illustrator: Julia LaPine
Paper/Printing: Two colors on Crane's Crest

American Pavilion

American Pavilion

American Pavilion Co., Inc. 1706 Warrington Avenue Danville, Illinois 61832

American Pavilion

American Pavilion Co., Inc.
1706 Warrington Avenue
Danville, Illinois 61832
217.443.0800
217.443.9619 Fax

American Pavilion

Tommy Thomas
Field Supervisor

American Pavilion Co., Inc. 1706 Warrington Avenue Danville, Illinois 61832 217.443.0800 217.443.9619 Fax

Client: Danville Tent & Awning
Design Firm: Sequel, Inc.
Art Director: Denise Olding
Designer: Denise Olding
Illustrator: Denise Olding
Paper/Printing: Two colors on Kimberly Writing Titanium White Wove

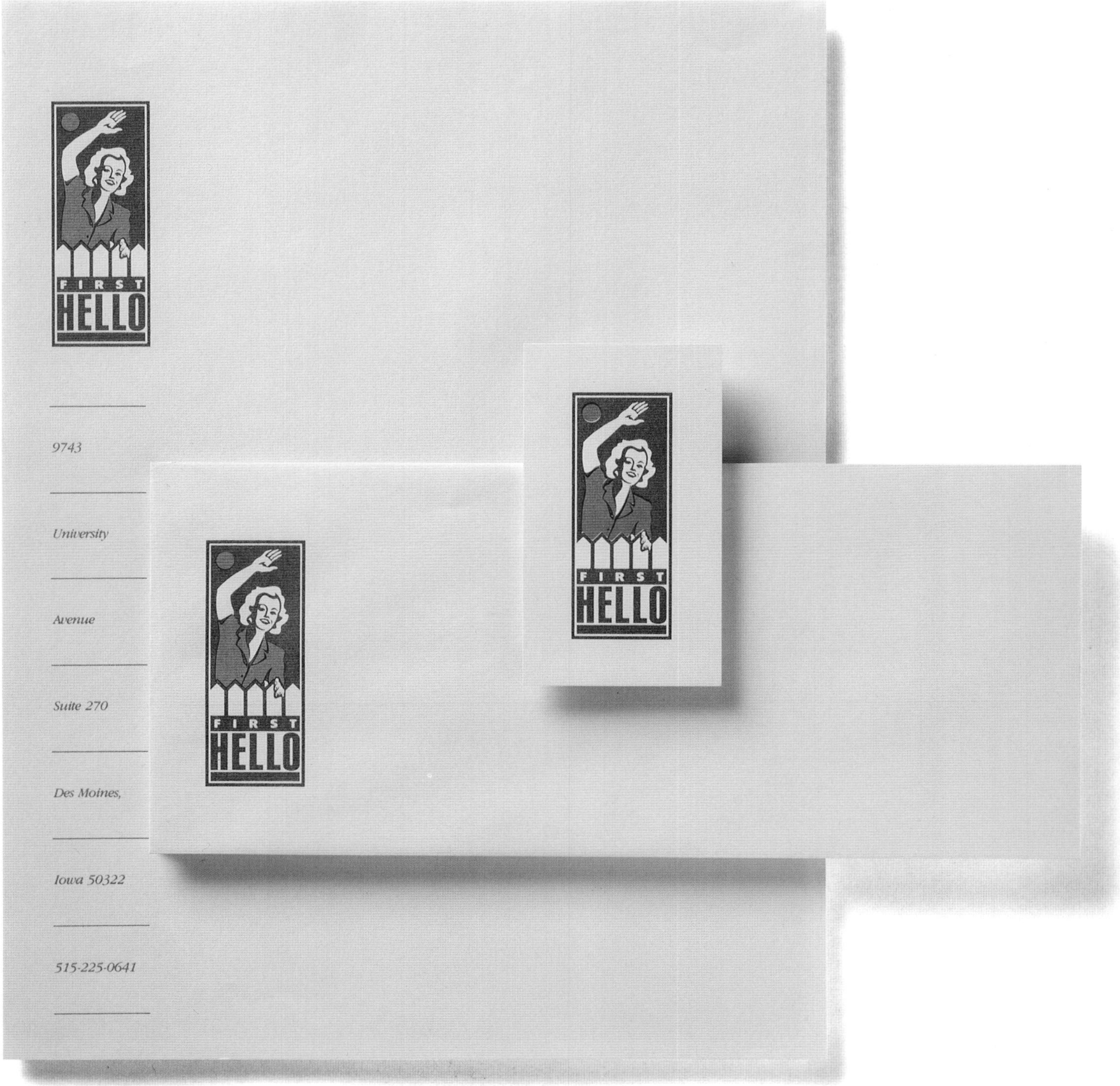

FIRST
HELLO
9743
University
Avenue
Suite 270
Des Moines,
Iowa 50322
515-225-0641
FIRST
HELLO
FIRST
HELLO

Client: First Hello
Design Firm: Sayles Graphic Design
Art Director: John Sayles
Designer: John Sayles
Paper/Printing: Two colors on Neenah Classic Crest

Client: Sarah Hall Clark
Design Firm: Clark Keller Inc.
Art Director: Jane Keller
Designer: Jane Keller
Illustrator: Frank Rawlings
Paper/Printing: Two colors on Speckletone

Client: Robert Heinrich
Design Firm: Steve Lundgren Graphic Design
Art Director: Steve Lundgren
Designer: Steve Lundgren
Paper/Printing: Two colors on Neenah Classic Crest

Client: Stacey Enterprises
Design Firm: Perich + Partners
Art Director: Ernie Perich
Designer: Janine Thielk, Carol Austin
Illustrator: Lyn Boyer-Penington
Calligraphy: Susan Skarsgard
Paper/Printing: Three colors on French Speckletone

Client: Crenshaw & Associates
Design Firm: Ashby Design
Art Director: Neal M. Ashby
Designer: Neal M. Ashby
Paper/Printing: Two colors on Simpson EverGreen Ash

ROWLAND AND ELEANOR BINGHAM MILLER

ROWLAND AND ELEANOR BINGHAM MILLER

3 Mockingbird Place
Louisville, Kentucky 40207
(502) 893-2262   (502) 587-6970

Client: Roland & Eleanor Bingham Miller
Design Firm: McCord Graphic Design
Art Director: Walter McCord and Eleanor Miller
Designer: Walter McCord
Illustrations: (ca. 1870) Courtesy Filson Club Archives
Paper/Printing: Four color process on Strathmore Alexandra Brilliant

P.O. Box 388
Clements
California 95227

209 759 3315

P.O. Box 388
Clements
California 95227

P.O. Box 388
Clements
California 95227

209 759 3315

Chris R. Dryden
Stallion Manager

Client: Blooming Hills Farm
Design Firm: Emery/Poe Design
Art Director: David Poe
Designer: David Poe
Illustrator: David Poe
Paper/Printing: Four colors on Strathmore Writing

Client: Amador Land & Cattle
Design Firm: Communication Arts Inc.
Art Director: Henry Beer
Designer: David A. Shelton
Paper/Printing: Two colors on Speckletone Ivory White Text

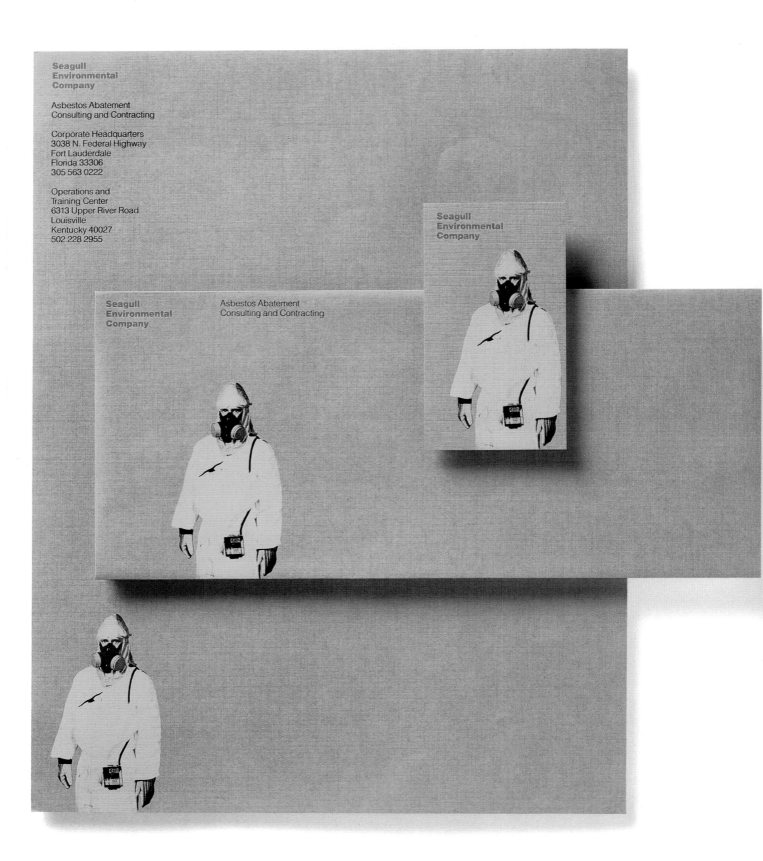

Seagull
Environmental
Company

Asbestos Abatement
Consulting and Contracting

Corporate Headquarters
3038 N. Federal Highway
Fort Lauderdale
Florida 33306
305 563 0222

Operations and
Training Center
6313 Upper River Road
Louisville
Kentucky 40027
502 228 2955

Seagull
Environmental
Company

Asbestos Abatement
Consulting and Contracting

Seagull
Environmental
Company

Client: Seagull Environmental Co.
Design Firm: McCord Graphic Design
Art Director: Walter McCord
Designer: Walter McCord
Paper/Printing: Three colors on Strathmore Rhododendron Smoke Grey

Client: Utah Yantis
Design Firm: Tollner Design Group
Art Director: Lisa Tollner
Designer: Kim Tucker
Illustrator: Kim Tucker
Paper/Printing: Two colors on Zanders Elephant Hide

CLEMENTE
McKAY
Funeral Homes

CLEMENTE
McKAY
Funeral Homes

CLEMENTE
McKAY
Funeral Homes

CYNTHIA M. CLEMENTE
FUNERAL DIRECTOR

700 Fifth St.
Struthers, OH 44471
(216) 755-1401

10170 Main St.
New Middletown, OH 44442
(216) 542-2060

Main Office
700 Fifth St. Struthers, OH 44471

700 Fifth St. Struthers, OH 44471
(216) 755-1401

10170 Main St. New Middletown, OH 44442
(216) 542-2060

Client: Clemente-McKay Funeral Homes
Design Firm: May Design Associates
Art Director: Frederick Mozzy
Designer: Frederick Mozzy
Illustrator: Frederick Mozzy
Paper/Printing: One color Strathmore Writing

Client: DLP International Inc.
Design Firm: Marc English: Design
Art Director: Marc English
Designer: Marc English
Paper/Printing: One color and embossing on Simpson Gainsborough

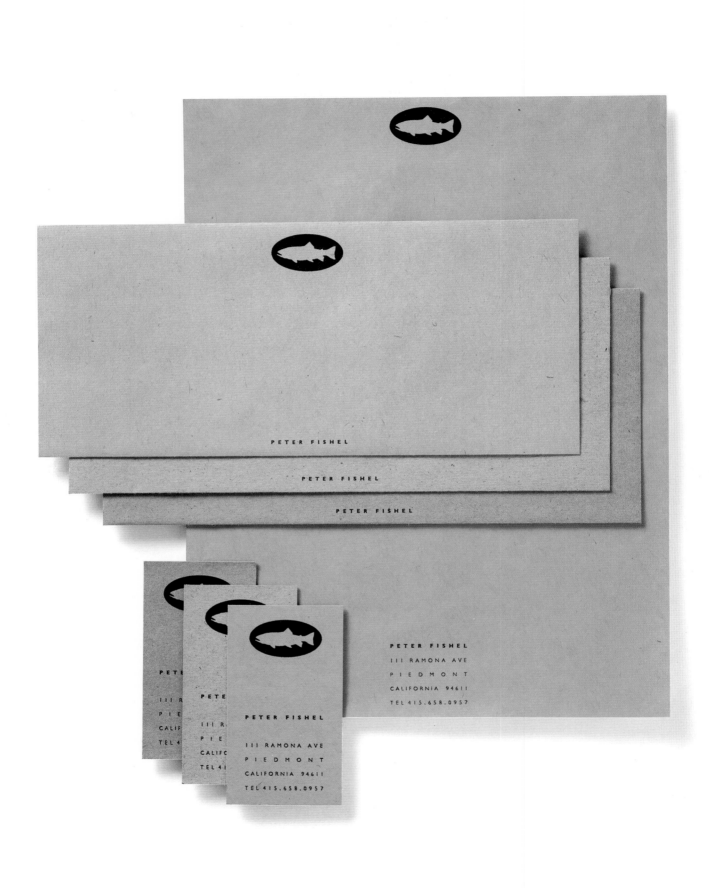

Client: Peter Fishel
Design Firm: Fishel Design
Art Director: Peter Fishel
Designer: Peter Fishel
Paper/Printing: Black (Xerox) on used grocery bags, butcher paper, etc.

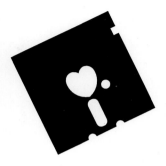

Client: Comdates
Design Firm: Kuo Design Group
Art Director: Samuel Kuo
Designer: Samuel Kuo

Client: Charlotte Heat
Design Firm: Design/Joe Sonderman, Inc.
Art Director: Joe Sonderman
Designer: Andy Crews

Client: Heitkamp Farms
Design Firm: Design Center
Art Director: Todd Spichke
Designer: Todd Spichke

Client: Video Jukebox Network
Design Firm: Ron Kellum Design
Designer: Ron Kellum
Illustrator: Ron Kellum

Client: Fox Broadcasting
Design Firm: Jerry Cowart Designers
Art Director: Jerry Cowart
Designer: David Westwood

Client: Rancho Encantado
Design Firm: Design Forum
Designer: Renae Roberts
Illustrator: Renae Roberts

14. INDEX

DESIGN FIRMS

DESIGN FIRM DIRECTORY

Adam, Fillippo & Associates
1206 Fifth Avenue
Pittsburgh, PA 15219

Alexander Isley Design
361 Broadway
Suite #111
New York, NY 10013-3903

Anthony McCall Associates
11 Jay Street
New York, NY 10013

Ashby Design
144 Duke of Gloucester Street
#4A
Annapolis, MD 21403

Barry David Berger + Associates
9 East 19th Street
New York, NY 10003

Bob Korn Design
370 1/2 Pacific Street
Brooklyn, NY 11217

Burns Connacher & Waldron
59 West 19th Street
Suite 4A
New York, NY 10011

CMC Design Associates
900 North Franklin
Suite 505
Chicago, IL 60610

Cipriani Kremer Design
2 Copley Place
Boston, MA 02116

Clarion Marketing and Communication
340 Pemberwick Road
Greenwich, CT 06927

Clark Keller Inc.
1160 Spa Road
Annapolis, MD 21403

Clifford Selbert Design
2067 Massachusetts Avenue
3rd Floor
Cambridge, MA 02140

Cognata Associates
1001 Bridge Way
#220
Sausalito CA 94965

Communication Arts Inc.
1112 Pearl Street
Boulder, CO 80302

Condon Norman Design
954 West Washington Blvd.
Chicago, IL 60607

Cordella Design
855 Boylston Street
Boston, MA 02116

Creative Works
631 U.S. Highway One
Suite 300
North Palm Beach, FL 33408

Culver & Associates
533 North 86th Street
Omaha, NE 68114

Davies Associates
5817 Uplander Way
Culver City, CA 90230

De Martino Design Inc.
584 Broadway
New York, NY 10012

Design Center
15119 Minnetonka Boulevard
Minnetonka, MN 55345-1508

Design Forum
3484 Far Hills Avenue
Dayton, OH 45429

Design/Joe Sonderman, Inc.
PO Box 35146
Charlotte, NC 28235-5146

Designed to Print + Associates, Ltd.
130 West 25th Street
New York, NY 10001

Designframe Inc.
One Union Square West
New York, NY 10003

Dinosaur Group Inc.
107 East 36th Street
New York, NY 10016

Donovan and Green
One Madison Avenue
New York, NY 10010

Douglas + Voss Group
201 East 16th Street
5th Floor
New York, NY 10003

Ellis • Pratt Design
452 Park Drive
Suite 20
Boston, MA 02215

Emery/Poe Design
330 Ritch Street
San Francisco, CA 94107

F. Eugene Smith Design Management
641 W. Market Street
Akron, OH 44303

Fishel Design
111 Ramona Avenue
Piedmont, CA 94611

Fitch Richardson Smith
139 Lewis Wharf
Boston, MA 02110

Flagg Brothers Inc.
Darien Executive House
397 Post Road
Darien, CT 06820

Frank D'Astolfo Design
80 Warren Street
#32
New York, NY 10007

Friday Saturday Sunday, Inc.
210 East 15th Street
New York, NY 10003

G.T. Rapp & Company
2815 Second Avenue
Suite 393
Seattle, WA 98121

George Tscherny, Inc.
238 East 72nd Street
New York, NY 10021

Greene Art Associates
216 West 18th Street
12th Floor
New York, NY 10011

Gunnar Swanson Design Office
739 Indiana Avenue
Venice, CA 90291-2728

Hafeman Design Group
935 West Chestnut
Suite 203
Chicago, IL 60622

Hornall Anderson Design Works
1008 Western Avenue
Floor 6
Seattle, WA 98104

Identity Center
1340 Remington Road
Suite Q
Schaumburg, IL 60173

Integrate, Inc.
503 South High Street
Columbus, OH 43215

Intelplex Design
12215 Dorsett Road
Maryland Heights, MO 63043

J. Brelsford Design, Inc.
1125 High Street
Des Moines, IA 50309

J.T. Taverna Associates Inc
344 M40 South
Allegan, MI 49010

Jack Tom Design
80 Varick Street
Suite 3B
New York, NY 10013

Janell Genovese Design
328 Washington Street
Somerville, MA 02143

Jerry Cowart Designers
22273 Del Valle Street
Woodland Hills, CA 91364

Jones Design & Advertising
31726 Rancho Viejo Road
Suite 207
San Juan Capistrano, CA 92675

Joseph Dieter Visual Communications
3021 Linwood Avenue
Baltimore, MD 21234

Josh Freeman/Associates
4222 Glencoe Avenue
Marina Del Ray, CA 90292-5612

Karen Schrader Design
10 Elm Road
Kings Park, NY 11754

Katz Wheeler Design
1219 Spruce Street
Philadelphia, PA 19107

Kevin P. Sheehan Design
8 Westland Avenue
Boston, MA 02115

Kollberg/Johnson Associates Inc.
7 West 18th Street
New York, NY 10011

Kuo Design Group
95 Fifth Avenue
New York, NY 10003

Lancaster Design & Art Inc.
10 Greenfield Road
Lancaster, PA 17602

Laurel Bigley Design
165 Diamond Street
Auburn, CA 95603

Lawrence Bender & Associates
512 Hamilton Avenue
Palo Alto, CA 94301

LeeAnn Brook Design
PO Box 1788
Nevada City, CA 95959

Letvin Design
119 Bellingham Avenue
Revere, MA 02151

Lewin/Holland Inc.
230 West 17th Street
New York, NY 10011

Lieber Brewster Corporate Design
324 West 87th Street
New York, NY 10024

Louise Fili Ltd.
22 West 19th Street
9th Floor
New York, NY 10011

M & Co.
50 West 17th Street
New York, NY 10011

M Plus M Incorporated
17 Cornelia Street
New York NY10014

McCord Graphic Design
2014 Cherokee Parkway
Louisville, KY 40204

Mace Messer Design Associates
311 Great Road
Littleton, MA 01460

Manhattan Design
47 West 13th Street
New York, NY 10011

Mark English: Design
57 Exeter Street
Arlington, MA 02174-3427

Margo Chase Design
2255 Bancroft Avenue
Los Angeles, CA 90039

Mark Palmer Design
41-994 Boardwalk
Suite A-1
Palm Desert, CA 92260

Marketing by Design
2212 K Street
Sacramento, CA 95816

May Design Associates
47 Federal Plaza
Youngstown, OH 44503

Michael Aron & Company
20 West 20th Street
New York, NY 10011

Michael Doret, Inc.
12 East 14th Street
New York, NY 10003

Michael Standard Inc.
1000 Main Street
Evanston, IL 60202

Milton Glaser Inc.
207 East 32nd Street
New York, NY 10016

Mortensen Design
627 Emerson Street
#200A
Palo Alto, CA 94301

Musser Design
558 Race Street
Harrisburg, PA 17104

Notovitz Design Inc.
47 East 19th Street
New York, NY 10003

Page, Arbitrio & Resen Ltd.
305 East 46th Street
New York, NY 10017

Page Design Inc.
1900 29th Street
Sacramento, CA 95816

Peggy Lauritsen Design
26 Hennepin Avenue
#209
Minneapolis, MN 55401

Perich + Partners Ltd.
552 South Main Street
Ann Arbor, MI 48104

Pollman Marketing Arts Inc.
2060 Broadway
#210
Boulder, CO 80302

Porter/Matjasich & Associates
154 West Hubbard
Suite 504
Chicago, IL 60610

Portfolio
38 Newbury Street
Boston, MA 02116

Puccinelli Design
114 East De la Guerra Street
Studio #5
Santa Barbara, CA 93101

Pushpin Group
215 Park Avenue South
New York, NY 10003

Qually & Company Inc.
30 East Huron
#2502
Chicago, IL 60611

Reiner Design
26 East 22nd Street
8th Floor
New York, NY 10010

Richard Danne & Asscoiates
126 Fifth Avenue
New York, NY 10011

Rick Eiber Design (RED)
4649 Sunnyside North
#242
Seattle, WA 98103

Robert Bailey Inc.
0121 SW Bancroft
Portland, OR 97201

Robert Cook Design
4803 Montrose Boulevard
Suite 11
Houston, TX 77006

Ron Kellum Design
1133 Broadway
Room 1214
New York, NY 10010

Rousso+Asociates, Inc.
5881 Glenridge Drive NE
K #200
Atlanta, GA 30328-5569

Rowe & Ballantine
8 Galloping Hill Road
Brookfield, CT 06804

Sally Johns Design Studio
1040 Washington Street
P.O. Box 10833
Raleigh, NC 27605

Sayles Graphic Design
308 Eighth Street
Des Moines, IA 50309

Sequel, Inc.
310 West Liberty
Louisville, KY 40202

Stark Design Associates
22 West 19th Street
9th Floor
New York, NY 10011

Steve Lundgren Graphic Design
6524 Walker Street
Suite 205
Minneapolis MN 55426

Stillman Design Associates
1556 Third Avenue
New York, NY 10128

Tharp Did It
50 University Avenue
Suite 21
Los Gatos, CA 95030

Thomas Nielson Design
678 Center Street
Newton, MA 02158

Tollner Design Group
111 North Market Street
Suite 1020
San Jose, CA 95113

Tracy Mac Design
2039 Griffith Park Boulevard
Los Angeles, CA 90039

Traver & Associates
424 Riverside Drive
Suite 203
Battle Creek, MI 49015

Turpin Design Associates
1762 Century Boulevard
Atlanta, GA 30345

Unlimited Swan, Inc.
272 Riverside Avenue
Riverside, CT 06878

Urban Taylor & Associates
12250 SW 131 Avenue
Miami, FL 33186

Vanderbyl Design
539 Bryant
San Francisco, CA 94107

WCVB TV Design
5 TV Place
Needham, MA 02192

Westwood & Associates
1230 Stanford Street
Santa Monica, CA 90404-1602

Whitmer Design
527 40th Street
Des Moines, IA 50312

Whitney • Edwards Design
3 North Harrison
PO Box 2425
Easton, MD 21601

William Homan Design
1316 West 73rd Street
Richfield, MN 55423-3007

Wilsonworks
1811 18th Street, NW
Washington, DC 20009